OUR DAILY BREAD

Other Books by the Author

A Book of Graces

A Book of Childhood Prayers and Verses

Our Daily Bread

Secrets from the Bakers of Cornwall

CAROLYN MARTIN

TABB HOUSE

First published in Great Britain 1993
Tabb House, 7 Church Street, Padstow,
Cornwall, PL28 8BG

ISBN 0 90718 99 8

Illustrations by Susan Cutting

Typeset by Exe Valley Dataset Ltd, Exeter, Devon
Printed and bound by the Short Run Press Ltd, Exeter, Devon

PREFACE

MY interest in the names for bread and cakes began many years ago when on holiday on the continent. Gazing into a particularly well-stocked *patisserie* window in Holland, dictionary in hand, I was able to translate some of the names for cakes as Goat's feet and Marrow bones. There are similarly bizarre names in Germany such as Ox eyes or Pig's ears, while in this country we have our Elephant's feet and Sardines in blankets.

Turning to Cornwall, I found that bakers and confectioners use many individual and confusing terms. A tea treat, for example, is a relation of the saffron bun. Yeast buns can be called dough buns, white saffrons or just white buns. These local and regional variations led me to research the names of bread and rolls within the county, from the Kazakhstan loaf in the far West of Cornwall, to the Turkestan in the East. Not only are individual breads baked in the South West, but the same loaf is often known by a different name. It was a fascinating trail of discovery.

ACKNOWLEDGEMENTS

VISITING the small bakers, and some of the not-so-small, in Cornwall has been a real pleasure. Not only have I been received with kindness and courtesy, but I have been inspired and encouraged by their enthusiasm and dedication. Many thanks to them and to those who generously gave their recipes, including Hogran Ltd, Abel and Schafer and Spiller's Premier Products Ltd.

Most have been willing to talk about their work and share their experiences. Indeed the fact that they have been so ready to explain the intricacies of the profession and give of their time may indicate that they are a neglected trade, some of our unsung heroes. They rise early, often starting work at 3.30 a.m., to ensure that fresh, warm and crusty bread is delivered to the shops by 8.0 a.m. The hours are long, the work is physically tiring and the bakeries can be unbearably hot in summer. Why do they do this? Perhaps running a bakery is within the reach of aspiring young entrepreneurs, although many bakeries are family businesses with third or fourth generation bakers. The opportunity for individualism and creativity is appreciated and many claim to enjoy the unsocial hours and would not move to other professions. In the main, bakers are men, but it is interesting to note that some young women bakers are now coming into the trade and running very successful bakeries and retail sales shops. The specialist bakery course at Cornwall College attracts both male and female applicants and when they finish their training, the opportunities are immense, with approximately three job vacancies for every qualified student.

My thanks are also due to my family, who have supported me in this enterprise and whose reward has been to sample the many delicious breads that I have made from the recipes in this book.

CONTENTS

MARKETING

OUR shopping habits have changed dramatically over the last fifty years, since World War II. No longer is the small local specialist the sole supplier; the village baker, butcher and grocer have been ousted by supermarkets, hypermarkets or superstores with their in-store facilities and lower priced loaves. Sunday opening and the high rents in town centres have also taken their toll and now many bakers have difficulty in surviving, particularly during the winter months in Cornwall. We all like the idea of the small, local trader, but only support them at our convenience. However, the high quality of service and the variety of excellent bread offered ensures that their goods and services are still in demand.

Another recent trend is for small corner shops to buy in stocks of frozen dough, which are then baked on the premises and sold to the customers as fresh bread the next morning. Butchers are becoming bakers, in an attempt to rescue their profits with the falling sales of meat.

Fortunately, statistics show that we buy most of our bread from supermarkets. The ease with which a wrapped, sliced loaf can be thrown into the freezer and then extracted when required, puts the small baker at a disadvantage. Price is the other consideration; mass produced factory loaves are naturally cheaper than individually moulded cottage loaves, which are labour intensive and therefore expensive to produce. All I can recommend is that we support our bakers before it is too late.

SOME TRADITIONAL NAMES FOR BREAD

SHOPPING for bread is a very individual business. Time and time again, when visiting bakery shops, I have overheard tongue-tied customers pointing to the particular loaf or cake of their choice, in an attempt to hide their ignorance and embarrassment at not knowing the local name.

The following national and Cornish names are in current use.

NATIONAL TERMS FOR LOAVES

Batch loaves are usually distinguished by soft sides, through being baked close together in the oven — although in Wales they like buns with crusty sides.

Bloomers, or **London bloomers** were introduced after World War I and were originally known as Victory loaves. They are moulded and baked on open sheets, long and dumpy in shape with short cuts along the top. The number of cuts varies depending on the whim of the individual baker. The name, according to some people, refers to the 'bloom' on the loaf, as it is taken out of the oven. The name is even attributed to Mrs Amelia Bloomer, the American who gave her name to cycling bloomers; the loaves are said to resemble bloomers when they lie on the trays prior to baking.

A cob is generally a round, brown loaf, often topped with cracked wheat. The term, I believe, derives from the old fashioned, derogatory name for a head. A hazelnut is also known as a cob and this may have a bearing on the name. There are also cob rolls.

A **coburg** is traditionally a round, white loaf with a cross cut across the top so that the loaf rises into a cauliflower shape. The cross is said to date from mediaeval times. The bread is a variation of the pan Coburg loaf, baked in a round shallow tin and allowed to rise into a soufflé shape. The name, as it suggests, comes from Germany.

A cottage loaf is well known, with a smaller dome of white dough that is placed on top of a larger mound as it proves. Although attractive in appearance, it has to be moulded by hand and as production is labour intensive it is expensive to make and has been phased out in many bakeries. The shape originates from Roman times, when the dough was moulded to fit into the beehive ovens.

Danish: the term is used to cover a wide variety of bread, from light slimming bread to a normal white dough, in a tin or oval shape. The main characteristic is that it is sprinkled with white flour before baking, which produces a white crisp crust.

A Farmhouse is usually a white, split tin loaf, but baked in a special tin so that the word Farmhouse appears on the side of the loaf. The top quarter of the loaf is allowed to rise and spread over the top of the tin, making the loaf somewhat squatter than the ordinary tin loaf. The top is invariably floured. During the last century, Farmhouse loaves were made with brown flour, to emphasise the health aspect in an attempt to move away from the general obsession with white bread.

French sticks are the well known long, thin loaves of white bread, weighing 16 oz. Baguettes are similarly shaped, but shorter and weighing just 12 oz. Napoleon is said to have first introduced the long French loaf. When on campaign in Russia in the winter of 1812, his troops complained about their diet of black bread. In response Napoleon arranged for special white bread to be baked, but every soldier had to carry his loaf in his pantaloons — hence the shape. Long loaves also allow maximum surface exposure for crusty baking.

Milk loaf is the name given to the circular ridged loaf, baked in a double cylindrical mould. Legally, it can only be called a milk loaf when it contains full cream milk. Throughout the country, it has a wide variety of names, from a crinkled or musket loaf to a rasp in Wales or a lodger in Shropshire. The latter term is used because the loaf is thought to be ideal for landladies, who can count the number of rings on the loaf and tell when the lodger creeps into the kitchen during the night to cut himself a slice. It can also be made into fancy shapes, such as a plait.

A sandwich loaf is generally oblong and as it is not allowed to rise in the oven, the top is flat. This result is obtained by upturning the tin as it is placed in the oven, to bake the loaf on the sole (floor) of the oven. Alternatively a flat tin is placed over the dough — hence the name underpan or undertin. When cut, the square slices are ideal for sandwich making.

A tin loaf and a split tin loaf are large white crusty loaves. The latter is distinguished by virtue of the long slash along the top of the loaf.

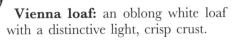

Vienna loaf: an oblong white loaf with a distinctive light, crisp crust.

ROLLS AND SPLITS

THESE are similarly divided into shape, size and flour type. Usually, white flour is used, but many rolls are now baked with wholemeal and granary flour. Within the trade, rolls, splits and croissants are known as 'morning goods'.

Baps and **Burgers** are round, squat, soft rolls, mainly used for beefburgers or savoury fillings. One supermarket packages the same product as burger buns in the winter and as salad baps during the summer months.

Bridge rolls are short, thin white rolls, the ideal accompaniment for bridge parties.

Finger rolls: longer than bridge rolls and useful for parties and mass catering.

Cobs and crusties: cobs are usually round buns with a crispy outer shell. Crusties tend to be longer, larger and torpedo shaped. Variations occur with such names as Vienna crusties, rustic French crusties or even oaties.

Splits: small, soft rolls in either white or brown flour. Traditionally, the main ingredient of a Cornish cream tea, thickly spread with home-made jam and topped with Cornish clotted cream. It is interesting to see that more people are asking for brown or even granary splits. In Devon and East Cornwall they are known as tuffs; definitely not spelt 'toughs'.

Other roll shapes are twists, spirals and swirls, knots, and rosettes as well as miniature cottage rolls.

SOME CORNISH VARIATIONS — LOAVES

A BATCH is usually a round loaf with soft sides, but it is a large, round crusty loaf in Falmouth, Bodmin, Newquay, Wadebridge and St Ives, whereas it is a short bloomer shape in Looe, Polperro, Liskeard and Redruth, with soft sides. In Kelly Bray, a batch has a very different shape, with an upturned end rather like a duck's tail. Then the students at Cornwall College bake a round, flat batch, made with slightly sweetened brown flour and this shape is repeated in Pensilva. In one shop in Liskeard, two kinds of batch are sold, one high and round and the other much lower and called a flat batch. A nearby baker also sells a tray batch, like a bloomer with soft sides and just three cuts across the top. Another variation can be found in Launceston, where a batch is more like a small tin loaf, with soft sides and decorated with short cuts.

Bloomers in Cornwall include a plaited bloomer, with a plait along its top, made in Lostwithiel.

Tin Loaves have an endless variety of names in Cornwall, from risers to humps, tops to uprights, with open, high, bold, round, oval or split tops in between. Probably the most original name is used in Penzance, where the goose loaf has a cut along the top of the loaf in the shape of a goose's tail feather. However, tin loaves are known as Long John's in Launceston — the only shop where Long John's lie alongside bloomers!

Sandwich loaves are known either as underpans or undertins in Cornwall. These names have an old fashioned, nostalgic ring about them and have been used by local people for many years. It is heartening therefore to see that the county has retained some individualism, despite the impact of tourist and the influx of residents from the Home Counties. Other names for these loaves are flat tops or squares. Fortunately the London name, cut loaf, has not yet crept into the vocabulary.

Milk loaves: the term can only be used when the bread contains full cream milk. Even so, customers generally know the round, barrel shaped loaf as a milk loaf though it can be called a concertina, rasp, square twist, bun loaf or ring. One bread shop in the north of the county does not have a name for it as such and accepts what customers decide to call it.

Novelty loaves such as the hedgehog are made at many different bakeries in Cornwall.

ROLLS AND SPLITS

SHORT, crusty rolls have a wide variety of names in Cornwall, from Vienna crusties in Falmouth, submarines or subs in Lelant, to torpedoes in Newquay. All these names are original and give an apt description of the product; the name nudger is used in Merseyside.

To quote Adrian Bailey in *The Blessings of Bread*, 'Bread shapes betray their origins, and many of these English loaves were born in the nineteenth century when the dough left the cottage hearth and came to town; some loaves are square because they have been baked in tins, while others, like the cob and cottage loaves, serve to remind the town-dweller that the countryside is not far away.'

CORNISH NAMES FOR DIFFERENT LOAVES

AREA NAMES FOR TIN LOAVES

Bold top	St Ives
Crown top	Boscastle
Crusty	Helston
Crusty top	Bodmin
Farmhouse	St Austell, St Dennis
Flat top	Bude
Goose loaf	Penzance
High	Polperro
High top	St Ives, Hayle
Hump top or Hump	St Mary's, Isles of Scilly
Large white upright	Liskeard
Long John	Launceston
Long tin	Padstow, Polperro, Callington, Launceston, Saltash
Open top	Newlyn
Oval top	St Columb Road, Callington
Riser	Redruth
Round top	Newquay
Split top	Falmouth
Split tin	Pensilva and other areas
Square tin	Saltash
Tall tin	Perranporth
Three quarter tin	Perranporth
Tin loaf	Perranporth, Nanpean and many other areas
Tops	Mullion
Upright	Camborne, Gunnislake, Kelly Bray, Bude
Upright tin	Liskeard, Callington, Launceston Saltash

AREA NAMES FOR SANDWICH LOAVES

Flat top	St Keverne, Isles of Scilly, Hayle, Helston
Long undertin	Liskeard
Square	Gunnislake, Lelant, Pensilva, Kelly Bray
Square underpan	Newquay
Underpan	Constantine, Newquay, Falmouth St Ives, Helston, St Austell, St Mawes, Nanpean, St Dennis
Undertin	Redruth, Camborne, Bude, Wadebridge, Rock, East Looe, Bodmin

AREA NAMES FOR BARREL-SHAPED MILK LOAVES

Bun loaf	St Columb Major
Concertina	Falmouth, Penryn, St Agnes, Bude
Fluted loaf	Wadebridge
Milk loaf	Penzance
Ring	Penzance, St Ives, Redruth
Square twist	St Just

Hevvas or Heavy cakes are not a type of bread but flat, dry fruit cakes with a criss-cross patterned top.

MAP (key opposite) showing names of large white loaves in different parts of Cornwall.

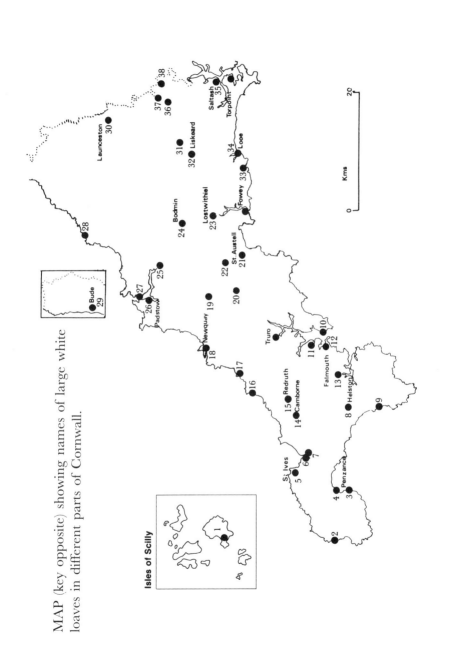

1. Isles of Scilly – Hump top, flat top
2. St Just – Square twist
3. Newlyn – Open top
4. Penzance – Goose loaf, milk loaf, ring
5. St Ives – Bold top, high top, ring, underpan
6. Lelant – Square
7. Hayle – Flat top, high top
8. Helston – Crusty, flat top, underpan
9. Mullion – Tops
10. St Mawes – Underpan
11. Penryn – Concertina
12. Falmouth – Concertina, split top, underpan
13. Constantine – Underpan
14. Camborne – Undertin, upright
15. Redruth – Ring, riser, undertin
16. St Agnes – Concertina
17. Perranporth – Tall tin, threequarter tin, tin loaf
18. Newquay – Round top, square underpan
19. St Columb – Bun loaf, oval top
20. St Dennis – Farmhouse, underpan
21. St Austell – Farmhouse, underpan
22. Nanpean – Tin loaf, underpan
23. Lostwithiel – Undertin
24. Bodmin – Crusty top, underpan
25. Wadebridge – Fluted loaf, undertin
26. Padstow – Long tin
27. Rock – Undertin
28. Boscastle – Crown top
29. Bude – Undertin, flat top
30. Launceston – Longjohn, long tin, upright
31. Pensilva – Split tin, square
32. Liskeard – Large white upright, long undertin, upright
33. Polperro – High, long tin
34. Looe – Undertin
35. Saltash – Long tin, square tin, upright tin
36. Callington – Long tin, oval top, upright
37. Kelly Bray – Square, upright
38. Gunnislake – Square, upright

AREA INDEX

Names in area headings in capitals

LIST OF RECIPES FROM THE BAKERS OF CORNWALL

13

Feast buns   75
  Nile, St Austell

French sticks   Polruan Bakery   106
Fruit and nut bread Par Bakery   77
Goose loaf   W.T. Warren & Son, St Just   26
Granary bread   S. Way & Sons, Grampound   61
Hanovian rye loaf   Oven Door Bakery, Penzance   31
Herb bread   Malcolm Barnecutt, Bodmin   80
Hovis loaf   J.H. & M. Choak, Falmouth   56
Irish soda bread   Penshell Bakery, Kilkhampton   93

Kazakhstan loaf   30
  Oven Door Bakery, Penzance

Kettle loaf   26
  W.T. Warren & Son, St Just

Kornknacker bread   49
  Horse and Jockey, Helston

Large riser   J.H. Glasson & Son, Redruth   38
Lincoln plum bread   Penshell Bakery, Kilkhampton   92
Malt loaf   Keith Barnecutt, Wadebridge   85

Saffron buns	Hot Bloomers Bakery, Callington	99
Saffron loaf	S.G. Greenaway, St Austell	74
Sage and celery seed rolls	Jane's Cake Shop, St Ives	35
Seed loaf	Mrs Hettie Merrick, Porthleven	48
Soda loaf	Kavorna Bakery, St Mary's	23
Soft grain bread	Polruan Bakery	106
Soft granary rolls	St Keverne Bakery	52
Sour dough	Ellery's Newquay	66
Splits	J.H. Glasson & Son, Redruth and	38
	Berryman's Bakery, Redruth	39
Subs	Matthews' Bakery, Lelant	34
Tiger topping	Martin's Bakery, St Austell	76
Top cobber jumbo rolls	St Agnes Bakery	45

Torpedoes   65
    The Bread Basket, Newquay

Traditional bun loaf Fresh N Crusty, St Austell   73

ORIGINAL TURKESTAN

Turkestan loaf   108
    Cawsand Bakery

Undertin	Laity's Bakery, Tuckingmill	40
Upright loaf	H. Pearce, Kelly Bray	98
Vienna loaf	Ellery's, Newquay	67
White bread	Tesco's, Truro	60
Vienna crusties	Cresta Bakery, Helston	50
Windmill loaf	Portreath Bakery	44

A NOTE ON THE RECIPES

BAKERS around the county have talked about many different kinds of bread to me, and those for which recipes are given in this book are underlined in the text. Naturally, over a period of time, changes and movements occur within the industry but, as far as possible, the information given here is correct at the time of going to press.

Our Daily Bread offers readers a unique slice of the baking scene within Cornwall during the 1990s and recipes which deserve to be preserved, remembered and used.

Bakers are accustomed to working in large quantities and the amounts may sometimes seem excessive, but whenever possible, the weights and measurements have been scaled down for domestic use. The recipes given in bulk will be of particular interest to bakers themselves.

Methods and descriptions have been given in the words of the bakers: sometimes the ingredients for different breads are similar but individual treatment makes each loaf unique. The measurements of water are extremely variable and I doubt whether many bakers actually measure the quantity used;they judge by experience. I usually allow at least $^1/_2$ pint of water for every 1lb of flour. Other variable factors are the warmth of the bakery and state of the oven. A full oven requires a higher temperature and a warm atmosphere encourages the yeast to grow. Most housewives know their own ovens and domestic ovens are usually set at slightly lower temperatures than the larger ovens within bakeries.

Both metric and imperial weights are given; exact conversion is difficult but a useful table is set out below. Approximate conversions are given in the individual recipes.

N B Litres and kilogrammes weigh the same
and 2lb = 1 pint, 13 fluid oz or 930 ml

SOLID MEASURES

$^{1}/_{2}$ oz	15 g
1 oz	25 g
2 oz	50 g
4 oz	100-125 g
8 oz	225 g
12 oz	350 g
16 oz	450 g
16-18 oz	500 g
32-36 oz	1 kg

LIQUID MEASURES

1 fl. oz	25 ml
2 fl. oz	50 ml
$^{1}/_{4}$ pint	150 ml
$^{1}/_{2}$ pint	250-275 ml
0.75	400-425 ml
1 p	550-575 ml
35 fl oz	1 litre

OVEN TEMPERATURES

F (Fahrenheit)	C (Centigrade)
250	130
275	140
300	150
325	160-170
350	180
375	190
400	200
425	210-220
450	230
475	240

GLOSSARY OF BAKERS' TERMS AND BAKERS' EQUIPMENT

Bay — hollow in flour for the liquid

Blend — mix in or combine

Clear — mix until the liquid is absorbed into the dough

Divider — machine for shaping and cutting dough

Dough temperature — room or container temperature for proving

Egg-wash — mixture of egg and milk, brushed over dough before baking

Ferment — allow yeast to develop and grow

French stick wire — long tray for baking French sticks

Improvers — Improvers are now permitted with wholemeal flour to help the bread to rise and then hold its shape. This is particularly critical when the dough is moved from the prover at the final stage into the oven.

Knock back — knead again after first rising, to redistribute the gas formed by the action of the yeast.

Mix to a crumb — mix until the mixture resembles bread-crunbs

Mixer — Several different industrial types of mixer are in use; at home, use a mixer with a dough hook, if available. Otherwise mix thoroughly, rubbing fat into the flour and kneading mixture well.

Mould — form dough into required shapes

Oven — Modern commercial ovens have very much thinner walls than old ones so that the heat cannot be turned off long before a batch of baking is finished, as used often to be the case. The fuller an oven, the greater the heat required. Usually at home, there is less in the oven and so a lower heat and shorter time can be used.

Peel — long handled wooden spade for removing bread from oven

Pin out — stretch and spread out dough on a flat surface

Prover — machine where bread is allowed to prove and rise; the home bread maker could use an airing cupboard, on top of a warm oven, etc.

Rest — allow to stand

Quick mix dough — dough that must be made quickly

Scale off — weigh out dough into required shapes and sizes

Small fermentation — ferment that takes place for a short time

Sole of oven — floor of oven

Sour dough — dough left until it has soured

Steam injection — give bread a burst of steam whilst baking

Tray up — place dough on baking trays

For further information on baking techniques, see the chapter on 'The Basics of Bread Making' at the end of this book.

I have myself baked the recipes with success and enjoyment — bon appetit!

THE ISLES OF SCILLY

BAKERS on the Isles of Scilly have particular problems; not only are they dependent on the weather for the delivery of fresh flour and yeast by sea, but having baked their bread, they then have to make sure that it is taken out to the off islands (the smaller islands) as quickly as possible. During the summer months they are inundated with orders and work long hours to keep up with demand. During the winter, custom is very slack and the hours shorter. A summer night shift begins at about 11 p.m., whereas a winter shift starts as late as 4.30-5 a.m. Most hotels and businesses on the Isles of Scilly have difficulty in recruiting seasonal staff and the bakeries are similarly under pressure through lack of suitably qualified workers.

There is only one retail bakery on St Mary's: the Kavorna Bakery, well situated in Hugh Street and probably visited by most holidaymakers at least once during their stay on the island. Mrs Elizabeth Parsons supervises operations and has been baking on the present premises since 1987. She employs 4-5 workers and organizes the orders and deliveries to customers on St Mary's as well as the off islands.

Names on the Isles of Scilly are slightly unusual, with large tin loaves being called hump tops or humps. Occasionally older people use the old-fashioned term hump back for a large white loaf. Sandwich loaves are flat tops or flats and the name hog or hedgehog is used for the popular short granary baton. A cheese and onion bread is baked regularly at the Kavorna Bakery and usually a soda loaf, which uses baking powder as the raising agent rather than yeast.

Other bakeries on the islands include Whittaker's wholesale bakery on the industrial estate in Hugh Town, which distributes to local shops but does not sell directly to the public. At one time St Agnes could proudly boast her own bakery, but this closed down in 1989. Surprisingly, on one of the smaller islands, Bryher, a small quantity of bread is baked by Mrs June Bushell at the Post Office. During the summer she can sell as many as 400 rolls a day, whereas in the winter the bread is only baked weekly.

SODA LOAF

*From Mrs Elizabeth Parsons, the Kavorna Bakery, St Mary's,
Isles of Scilly*

Ingredients
1 lb (450 g) white flour
4 level tsp. baking powder
1 oz (25 g) margarine
1 tsp salt
10 fl oz (250g) milk

Method Mix dry ingredients to a crumb, then fold in milk to make a soft dough. Work into a round and mark into four sections.

Bake at 400 F for 30 mins.

PENWITH

SURPRISINGLY, the largest bakery chain in the county is based in the far west of Cornwall, in wild, windswept Penwith. From their factory at St Just, Mr Brian Warren and his son Jonathan distribute their bread to most of the major towns in Cornwall, from Penzance to Plymouth. Established in 1860, W.T. Warren and Son must be one of the oldest bakeries in the county, and the organization involved in distributing bread over such a wide area has to be admired. The range of bread baked by Warrens is extensive, with such old-fashioned lines as the *kettle loaf* and the *goose loaf* for the Penzance area, as well as more recent additions such as rye bread and a twin loaf — two small tin loaves baked together, to enable pensioners to buy one at a time if they so wish. As a concession to Devonians, their splits are known as tuffs in the area around Plymouth.

Like David in the shadow of Goliath, Mrs Butters at the Pendeen Steam Bakery bakes her bread for customers in the immediate vicinity. Following her late husband's father and grandfather, Mrs Butters is the third generation of bakers in Pendeen. Her husband's grandfather started the business with a delivery basket and then built a bakery close to the school; baking has taken place on the present bakery premises since 1910. Even today, many of the old bakery mixers and bread tins are still used.

The variety of bread produced is small, but the bakery makes up for this by catering for individual requirements. One such example is the recipe given for pure bread, initially made especially for a customer who could not digest any additives or preservatives.

PURE BREAD

From Mrs W.J. Butters, The Steam Bakery, Pendeen

A quick recipe with just one rising, producing a most acceptable, well risen everyday white loaf.

Ingredients

$3^1/_2$ lb (1.575 kg) untreated flour

1 oz (25 g) salt

$^3/_4$ oz (20 g) vegetable cooking fat

$^1/_4$ oz (5 g) sugar

2 oz (40 g) yeast

2 lb (900 g) water, depending on the density of the flour
  (N B: 2lb = 1 pint,13 fluid oz or 930 ml)

Makes 5 **x** 1lb or 400g loaves

Method Mix and then prove in warmth for 30 mins.

Bake for 25 mins. at 450 F.

GOOSE LOAF and KETTLE BREAD

Both loaves are made from the same mixture of white dough
This and the following recipe are given by the head baker,
Mr Peter Polmear, at W.T. Warren and Son, St Just.

Ingredients
2lb 3oz (975 g) bread (strong white) flour
0.75oz (20 g) salt
$1^{1}/_{4}$ oz (40 g) yeast
$1^{1}/_{2}$oz (40 g) lard
0.75-1 pint (425-550 ml) water warmed to 65-75°
Method Make up dough. Stand for $1^{1}/_{2}$ hours. Knock back, stand a further three quarters of an hour and scale into dough pieces. Bake at 450 F for 50 mins.

RYE BREAD

Ingredients
1lb 12 oz (800 g) bread flour
1lb 12 oz (800 g) rye flour
1oz (25g) salt
1 oz (40 g) black treacle
1oz (25g) fat
$1^{1}/_{2}$ oz (40 g) yeast
Approx. 1lb 12oz (800 g) water
Method as above, but note the addition of treacle.

PENZANCE

IN Penzance local names abound, and long may they remain. The split tin loaf is curiously called a goose loaf — the cut is supposed to represent a goose's tail feather — mansion loaves are made from a straightforward white dough, but this is then rolled and folded into a distinct baton shape. Kettle loaves are similar to cottage loaves in size, but baked in a round, fluted tin with a lid to prevent rising, giving a squat loaf, with an attractive edge. The name stems from the Cornish kettle or cover, which used to be placed over the dough as it baked on a griddle within the Cornish peat or wood fire. Kettle bread was originally made from barley meal and sour dough, although later it was prepared with buttermilk and soda, rather like an Irish sweet bread. The custom of cooking bread in this way continued until late into the nineteenth century, but today it is only produced by a few bakeries in West Cornwall. As one baker pronounced, it is wasteful for sandwich making and sliced loaves are preferred.

In the town of Penzance, the bread scene is dominated by Mr Don Job from the Oven Door Bakery and perhaps he can be called the king of small bakers in West Cornwall. He is well known within the profession for his wide range of bread (68 varieties) and his skill in producing intricate pastillage (sugar sculpture) decorations for local and national competitions. Mr Job learnt his trade in South Wales, but he moved to Cornwall sixteen years ago and since then he has introduced many new names and varieties to the area. For any bread enthusiast, Penzance clearly is the place to visit.

Mr Job is said to have introduced the name goose loaf to the area, as well as the leopard loaf — a bloomer-type loaf, dusted with a rice flour mixture to give a distinctive speckled topping. The exact ingredients for the finish are a closely guarded secret; other bakers have tried to imitate the topping, but without success. The definitive recipe remains with Mr

Job. Smaller versions are baked and appropriately called leopard cubs and tiger baps.

Mr Job bakes four types of rye bread: dark Bavarian rye made with 60% rye flour, which keeps well; Scandinavian rye made with a lighter flour; *pain de seigle* (*seigle* is the French word for rye), a well baked, dark loaf; and *Hanovian rye* (formerly known as caraway rye) which has an impressive list of ingredients including hazelnuts, sultanas and walnuts. Four varieties of wholemeal bread are baked and at weekends customers can choose novelty breads, such as crocodiles, hedgehogs or tortoises. Other unusual breads baked are oatmeal with rye, twinnies and the unique *Kazakhstan loaf.*

Penzance has other bread shops, which as expected are busy during the summer months, but quiet during the winter. Andrews Hot Bread Shop in Albert Street has a brisk trade owing to the prominent position of the shop, but the types of bread are straightforward, with large or small white loaves, wholemeal or granary.

In nearby Newlyn, Mr Frank Eddy is the third generation of bakers to work in the Jack Lane Bakery, which is tucked away in a narrow, steep street above the town. The business was started by his grandfather in 1918 and the present Mr Eddy has been baking now for 40 years. He regrets that the old-fashioned loaves are no longer in great demand, but he still bakes *mansion* and kettle loaves for older customers. Two small loaves baked together are called dividers and the large tin loaf is known as an open top loaf in Newlyn. Individual customer requirements are catered for; Mr Eddy regularly makes to order a twist, which is a French stick knotted in the centre. At his bakery heavy cakes are known as hevvas, the original Cornish term.

MANSION LOAF

From Mr Frank Eddy at the Jack Lane Bakery, Newlyn.

Although basically a plain white dough, the loaf is shaped and moulded into a baton, with one end of the loaf higher than the other. According to Mr Eddy, the loaf was originally baked for the French sailors who regularly called in at the port. The French liked a larger version, but the locals prefer the smaller loaf.

Ingredients

4 lbs (1.800 kg) flour
$1^{1}/_{4}$ oz (30 g) salt
2 oz (50 g) yeast
2 oz (50 g) white fat
2 pints (1.1 litre) water

Method Add warm water to flour, salt, yeast and fat. Rest for 30 minutes, knock back well. Rest for 30 minutes and mould to shape. The moulding is all-important; the dough is rolled flat, then folded over with a distinct fold in the centre of the dough. The mixture is then rolled into a baton shape and baked on a sheet.

Bake at 450 F (for 2lb size) for approx. $^{3}/_{4}$ hour. The temperature depends on how much is in the oven; if it is full of fresh dough, the temperature has to be higher. If fairly empty, then the temperature is lower.

KAZAKHSTAN LOAF

This and the following recipes are from Mr Don Job,
The Oven Door Bakery, Penzance.

The name is a variation of the Turkestan loaf, marketed in the Plymouth area. The dough contains an impressive list of ingredients, with numerous varieties of seeds and nuts, giving a unique nutty flavour. Note — the loaf does not contain fat.

Ingredients

60 lb (27.00 kg) organic wholemeal stoneground flour
10 lb (4.50 kg) mixture of the following: millet seed, rye flour, sunflower seeds, kibbled wheat, sesame seeds, maw seeds
$1^1/_4$ lb (560 g) salt
2 lb (900 g) yeast
$5^1/_2$ gallons (approx. 25.130 litres) water
20 lb (12.60kg) mixture of the following ingredients: ground hazelnuts, roasted ground hazelnuts, flaked hazelnuts, roasted nibbed hazelnuts, flaked almonds, toasted coconut, kibbled walnuts, roasted whole hazelnuts, nibbed peanuts.

Method Mix ingredients together and scale off into 1 lb or 450 g pieces. Leave to prove until the dough reaches the top of the tin. As the mixture is so heavy, it will not rise a great deal. Roll the dough in the following mixture before baking.

28 lb (12.60 kg) flaked hazelnuts
14 lb (6.30 kg) polished sesame seeds
2 lb (900 g) maw seeds
$^1/_2$ lb (225 g) caraway seeds
28 lb (12.60 kg) nibbed hazelnuts or peanuts

Bake 30-35 minutes at 450 F.

HANOVIAN RYE

A dark, wholesome and satisfying loaf.
Ingredients
55 lb (24.75 kg) rye flour
15 lb (6.75 kg) organic wholemeal flour
1¼ lb (660 g) salt
1 lb (450 g) vegetable oil
2 lb (900 g) high activity yeast
A small quantity of ascorbic acid (vitamin C) is optional
At least 5 gallons of water
Then mix together
28 lb (12.60 kg) hazelnuts
14 lb (6.30 kg) whole roast hazelnuts
7 lb (3.15 g) sultanas (Crown Australian)
7 lb (3.15 g) walnuts
Add 14 lb of this mix to the top ingredients
Method Mix all ingredients well together; the dough should be quite sticky. Leave to prove in baskets or tins for 20-25 minutes. Brush with water and sprinkle with sesame and caraway seeds.
Bake at 450-475 F for ¾ hour.

ST IVES AND LELANT

THE area is well served with a good cross-section of small bakers, from the traditional Ferrel family bakers in busy Fore Street, St Ives, to the more recently established Matthews' bakery in Lelant. In Lelant, customers can buy an interesting selection of rolls or large baps shaped by hand as well as a variation on torpedoes — long crusty rolls — called *subs*. Ferrell's bakery is run by David and Margaret Ferrell and many of the recipes that they use have been handed down from their grandfather, Samuel Ferrell. Sales are extremely busy during the summer months and when they have time, they bake some of the more old-fashioned breads, such as crown or mansion loaves.

Jane's Cake Shop in Ayr, St Ives specialises in miniature novelty cakes, Cameo Cakes and these are marketed at home and abroad. As a sideline Jane Furneaux also offers some unusual rolls, *sage and celery*, sunflower or sesame seed rolls. These are popular with tourists during the summer.

Tucked away behind the main street, Mr J. Thomas in Street an Pol bakes for the locals rather than tourists and the fittings in the shop have been deliberately retained to give an old-fashioned appearance. Mr Thomas has been baking on the present premises for 34 years and his family have been bakers in St Ives for 70 years. Regretfully, Mr Thomas is due to retire shortly. One usual recipe offered by Mr Thomas is his wholemeal *farl loaf*, a bread usually associated with Ireland.

Other bakers in the area include the Uppercrust Bakery in Street an Garrow, St Ives and Philps Bakery, Foundry Square, Hayle. Both bakeries sell large, flat burger baps which seem to be a speciality of the area. Speckled tiger baps can be bought at the Uppercrust Bakery and Philps use the term Canadian wholemeal for their large wholemeal loaves. Here, large tin loaves are called high tops or just highs.

FARL LOAF

From Mr John Thomas, J. and J. Thomas, Street an Pol, St Ives

A round, wholemeal loaf, cut into four segments.

Ingredients

$3^{1}/_{2}$ lb (1.575 kg) wholemeal flour
$^{3}/_{4}$ oz (20 g) yeast
$1^{1}/_{2}$ oz (40 g) lard
$^{3}/_{4}$ oz (20 g) salt
$1^{1}/_{2}$-2 pints (.825-1.1 litres) water

Method Mix flour, salt and lard in bakers' conventional mixer, second speed for 10-15 minutes, before adding yeast and water. Prove in mixer for 10 minutes before knocking back and shaping into round farls, cut into four segments. Place on trays in the prover for about $^{1}/_{2}$ hour; again, the timing is estimated. The baker knows when the bread is ready for the oven; over proving is just as disastrous as under proving, as both cause the loaf to shrink in the oven. Mr Thomas usually takes the loaves out of the prover when they have reached about 90% of the required size.

Bake at 450° for 30-35 minutes.

N B Although the quantity of yeast in the recipe is low, the desired result is obtained by the long proving time. Additional yeast would accelerate rising.

SUBS

From Mr Mike Matthews, Matthews' Bakery, Lelant

Subs are long submarine-shaped brown rolls. In other areas, these rolls are called torpedoes.

Ingredients

32 kilo bag of flour — Harvester, white or 100% wholemeal
1 lb (450 g) salt
2 lb (900 g) yeast
1¼ lb (560 g) vegetable fat
Approx. 2 gallons (9 litres) of water, depending on the density
 of the flour

Method Mix all ingredients for 12 minutes in spiral mixes, 2 minutes on slow and 10 minutes on fast. Divide into required sizes, 3½-4oz weight, put into prover for 35-40 minutes.
Bake for 12-20 minutes at 425°.

SAGE AND CELERY SEED ROLLS

From Jane Furneaux, at Jane's Cake Shop, St Ives

Method Add 1 teaspoon of celery seeds and 2 teaspoons of dried sage to every 14 oz of white or brown dough.

CAMBORNE AND REDRUTH

THIS is an area with many small, traditional bakeries and an abundance of local names. Even the traditional rivalry between the towns of Camborne and Redruth extends into bread names, with the term riser being used in Redruth for the tin loaf, with variations on large, small, brown or white risers. Nearby in Camborne, the name upright or even an overtin is preferred. Just to be different again, the sandwich loaf is an undertin in Camborne and the traditional bloomer shaped loaf is often known as a batch. The *undertin* recipe given is from Laity's Bakery in Tuckingmill.

The Glasson family have been bakers in Redruth since 1916, but sadly the bakery closed during the summer of 1991. The ovens in the bakery had been in use for many years and were second hand when they were installed in 1962. We are privileged, though, to be able to give Mr Glasson's family recipes for splits and a *large riser*. Mr Williams from Marks in Camborne offers his recipe for the *cobber loaf*, round in shape and made with granary flour. Leopard loaves are also sold at Marks and they have an unusual variety of small rolls, with seedy knots, cottage rolls, Scotch baps (triangular in shape) and cobber rolls. Berryman's main bakery is in Redruth, but their shop window in Camborne is well worth viewing: the bread and rolls are elegantly displayed in old-fashioned wicker baskets, a delightful snub to modern shop fittings. Mrs Berryman gives us another version of Cornish *splits* in her well-tried family recipe.

Cornwall College at Pool is situated between the two areas. Here an imaginative range of bread is baked and sold to the public by the students from the specialized bakery course. A Swansea pilot is a white, oven bottom bread in the shape of a rugby ball, whereas a *press pin cob* is the same basic dough, but rather like a coffee bean, with a long fold down the centre. The batch loaf baked at the College is flat and round, dark in colour and sweet to taste. The ideal bread to serve at dinner parties.

LARGE RISER

From Mr Glasson, J.H. Glasson and Son, Redruth

Ingredients

70 lbs (31.50 kg) white unbleached flour
$1^1/_4$ lbs (560 g) salt
8 oz (225 g) lard
1lb (450 g) sugar
$1^1/_4$ lb (560 g) yeast
Water to mix — the baker knows the amount from
  experience.

Method Mix in spiral mixer for 2 minutes on slow and 8 minutes on fast. Prove for 1 hour. Scale off into tins and leave for $^1/_2$-$^3/_4$ hour. Bake $^1/_2$-1 hour, depending on the heat of the oven and what else is baking at the same time and whether the oven is full. Temperature 450-500 F.

CORNISH SPLITS

These can also be baked with wholemeal or granary flour. In the latter case, the milk powder is omitted.

Ingredients

$3^1/_2$l bs (1.575 kg) flour
1 oz (25g) salt
1 oz (25 g) milk powder
$1^1/_2$ oz (40 g) granulated sugar
4 oz (100 g) lard
2 oz (50 g) yeast
Water — at the baker's discretion

Method Mix in spiral mixer for 2 minutes on slow and 8 minutes on fast. Rest for half an hour in 4 lb quantities and then scale into splits, using the moulder and divider. Again, leave to rise and prove for $^1/_2$ hour. Bake at 450 F or even 500 F, depending on the oven. Time is variable, Mr Glasson says that he just looks into the oven and knows when they are done.

CORNISH SPLITS

From Mrs Lilian Berryman at Berryman's Bakery, Redruth

This well-tried family recipe uses a wet dough, producing light, sweet splits, a real advertisement for Cornish cream teas.

Ingredients
1 lb (450 g) strong white flour
1 oz (25 g) margarine
$^1/_4$ oz (10 g) salt
$^1/_2$ oz (15 g) milk powder
$^1/_2$ oz (15 g) yeast — with a minimum of sugar to assist rising
$^1/_2$ pint (250 ml) water

Method Mix all the dry ingredients for 4 minutes before adding the water and yeast. Add water and yeast and wet mix for 12 minutes. Leave to bulk prove for 5 minutes. Weigh off into 1lb lumps before using the machine to shape into splits. Prove again for 30-40 minutes before baking.

Bake for about 10 minutes at 420 F.

UNDERTIN

From Mr Roger Laity at Laity's Bakery, Tuckingmill, Camborne

This is Mr Laity's favourite loaf and one supermarket bakery manager told me that he always comes to Tuckingmill to buy his white bread from Laity's Bakery. The ingredients and method are the same for a white riser.

Ingredients
70 lbs (31.50 kg) unbleached, untreated white flour
1$^{1}/_{2}$ lbs (680 g) salt
1$^{1}/_{2}$lbs (680 g) vegetable fat
1$^{1}/_{2}$lbs (680 g) yeast
Approx. 4 gallons (18 litres) water

Method Mix in dough mixer for 20 minutes. Leave to rest for $^{1}/_{2}$ hour. Scale off into 400 and 800 g weights. Leave to rise again for half an hour.

Bake for 40 minutes at 450 F.

COBBER LOAF

From Mr H. Williams at Marks in Camborne

A round cob-shaped loaf, at one time made with cobber flour, but now with granary flour. Cobber flour is a granary type of flour, but rather moister.

Ingredients

4 lbs (1.8 kg) granary flour
2 oz (50 g) salt
2 oz (50 g) lard
Approx. 2 lb (900 g) water
2 oz (50 g) yeast

Method Rub fat and salt into flour. Pile flour onto working surface and make a bay in the centre, dissolve the yeast in the water and gradually add the water to the flour and mix in. The quantity of water is variable and it is best to mix in $3/4$ and then add the last $1/4$ if necessary. Prove for half an hour, knock back and mould into 1lb cobs. These should be a hand-span of $5^1/2$ inches in diameter. Dust with flour and prove before **baking** at 440 F for 45 minutes. The longer baking time gives a good crusty topping.

PRESS PIN COB

*From Mr M. Williams, who heads the bakery course at
Cornwall College*

The shape of this loaf is very unusual, like a coffee bean, and
the effect isobtained by dividing the dough with a rolling pin
and then proving on its side.

Ingredients

2 lbs (900 g) strong white bread flour
$^1/_2$ oz (15 g) salt
$1^1/_2$ oz (35 g) yeast
$^1/_2$ oz (10 g) sugar
1.75 lbs (600 g) water
$^1/_2$ oz (15 g) milk powder
The quantities are sufficient for 3 loaves.

Method Mix dry ingredients together. Disperse yeast in
warm water. Stream water into bowl and mix on slow for 1
minute then on second speed for 2-3 minutes, until a bright,
clear dough is obtained. Allow to ferment for 1 hour, knocking back after 40 minutes. Scale at 460 g and mould into
rounds. Rest for 10 minutes. Press lightly oiled rolling pin
from top to base of round, not quite separating. Prove dough
on its side, so that a coffee bean shape is obtained. If the
dough is proved flat, the two halves would separate or fall too
widely.

Bake Turn upright on tray to bake, for 30 minutes at 235 C.

PORTREATH AND ST AGNES

THERE is just one bakery in Portreath, run by an enthusiastic young baker and confectioner, Marion Halling, who also teaches part-time to students on the Bakery Course at Cornwall College. Baking is done at the back of the shop and the limited size of the premises restricts the output. Mrs Halling is hoping to expand her business and has ideas for moving into other areas. Twenty workers are employed in the summer and just four fewer during the winter.

You have to be up early to buy the bread of your choice in Portreath; customers are queuing before 8 a.m. and many lines are sold out by 9. Visitors come to buy bread on a regular basis from Penzance and some come from as far afield as Bristol and Scotland! Unusually, the bread is not displayed in the shop window, but is laid out attractively in traditional baskets within the shop. An extensive range of bread is on offer, but the names are fairly standard, although there is beige bread, a mixture of white and wholemeal flour, and speckle bread, white bread sprinkled with sunflower seeds, rustic and veggie bread for vegetarians. One favourite in the village is the *granary windmill*.

Situated in the centre of St Agnes village is St Agnes Bakery, small and old fashioned, with a sign outside the shop boasting that there has been a bakery here since 1905. Much of the equipment has been used since that time; wooden dough troughs and antique scales, for example. The bakery is now run by Mrs Sue Sneddon.

Holidaymakers frequent the shop and the local hotels and public houses are well served with such items as *top cobber jumbo rolls*, for ploughman's lunches or as filled rolls. Brown splits are also a speciality; some visitors insist on calling them bread cakes. It is interesting to note, too, that the kettle loaf from the West of Cornwall is still made in St Agnes; this is a white dough baked in a fluted tin with another tin placed on top of the dough to prevent rising during baking.

GRANARY WINDMILL LOAF

From Mrs Marion Halling at Portreath

THIS recipe has no connection with the well-known proprietary brand, but is a flat, circular bread made with granary dough and then cut into six or eight sections.

Ingredients

3 lb 8 oz (1.575 kg) granary flour

1½ oz (40 g) yeast

1 oz (25 g) salt

½ oz (15 g) lard

Approx. 32 fluid oz (800 ml) warm water

The quantities make about 5 loaves

Method Mix together the flour, salt and fat. Disperse yeast through the water and add to the above. Make up into dough. Cover with a damp cloth in a draught-free place. After 40 minutes, knock back and then rest for 20 minutes. Scale into 1 lb pieces. Mould round and rest 5-10 minutes. Roll into 9 inch rounds, flatten and mark into 6 pieces. Dust with granary flour.

Bake in a pre-heated oven at 232 C or 450 F for 30-35 minutes.

TOP COBBER JUMBO ROLLS

From Mrs Sue Sneddon at St Agnes Bakery

Mrs Sneddon has all her recipes written out by hand in a
well-worn recipe book and she uses vegetable fat rather than
animal, to cater for vegetarians.

Ingredients

$3^3/_4$ lb (1.69 kg) cobber flour
$^3/_4$ oz (20 g) salt
$^3/_4$ oz (20 g) malt
$^1/_2$ oz (15 g) vegetable fat
$1^1/_2$ oz (40 g) yeast
$1^1/_2$ pints (825 ml) water

Method Mix until the dough clears the mixer, for about 10
minutes. Divide into individual rolls and prove for 30
minutes, in trays. Bake at 500 F for 20 minutes.

N B Give the dough just one rising.

HELSTON AND THE LIZARD

GENERALLY, Helston and the Lizard are poorly served with shops and supermarkets but the number and range of small bakeries is quite heartening. In the town of Helston, both Rowe's and Warren's have their own bread shops and Mullion Bakery and Mr Don Job from The Oven Door Bakery in Penzance sell their bread and rolls in Ruth's Café, in Meneage Street. Almost opposite, Miss Juliet Vingoe has a flourishing business selling bread and cakes to the tourists and Helstonians, with such wholesome delicacies as carrot cake, sunflower rye and unusual kornknacker bread. The latter has created so much curiosity amongst the customers that the ingredients are displayed on the counter for all to see.

On the outskirts of the town, Mr Tonkin heads the Cresta Bakery on the curiously named Water Ma Trout Industrial Estate, (apparently called after a man named Trout and a corruption of the Cornish for Trout's mine). A baker with many years of experience, Mr Tonkin can remember the old-fashioned breads and flours and regrets the passing of such names as Turoq, Bermaline, Youma and Procea. He has shops in Porthleven and Constantine and sells as far away as Falmouth. Here his Dusty Miller loaf, a short bloomer-shaped white loaf dusted liberally with flour, is said to be called after Mr Miller, the proprietor of the Albany Stores, Lister Street, Falmouth, where the bread is sold. Mr Tonkin personally prefers his own *Vienna crusties*, with a crisp flaky crust, and says that they are delicious split and buttered.

Further south down along the Lizard, there is the St Keverne Bakery to the East and Mullion Bakery to the West. Both sell to shops, hotels and public houses in the area, giving the residents and tourists good supplies and service. In Mullion, large white tin loaves are called tops whereas sand-wich loaves in St Keverne are known locally as flat tops. Recipes for *Chinese Bread* from Mullion and *soft granary rolls* from St Keverne are given below.

Before leaving the Helston area, Mrs Hettie Merrick, from An Gegyn in Porthleven should be mentioned. Although not strictly a baker, until quite recently she ran the pasty and cake shop close to the picturesque harbour in Porthleven, where, according to one culinary expert, the best pasties in Cornwall can be found. The business has recently been taken over by Mr and Mrs S. Denness but the traditional lines are continued. Customers come from far and wide to sample the large, wholesome traditional Cornish pasties or the liver and onion, cheese or vegetable varieties. As well as pasties, Mrs Merrick specializes in Cornish cookery and her book *Pasties and Cream*, with recipes and local history, can be purchased in the shop. Whilst watching the pasties being made or waiting for them to cook, customers can choose from a range of Cornish cakes and buns and Mrs Merrick's recipe for *seed loaf* is given.

SEED LOAF

From Mrs Hettie Merrick, An Gegyn, Porthleven

Ingredients
1 lb (450 g) strong flour
Pinch salt
$^1/_2$ oz (15 g) yeast
$2^1/_2$ oz (65 g) Trex (lard)
$3^1/_2$ oz (90 g) margarine
2 oz (50 g) sugar
1 egg
$^3/_4$ oz (20 g) caraway seeds, according to taste
Approx. $^3/_4$ cup of milk
Method Whisk yeast into a little milk. Place flour and salt
into a bowl. Rub fats into flour, add sugar and caraway seeds.
Pour in yeast liquid, eggs and remainder of milk and stir with
a knife to mix, then knead well. Cover dough with a cloth
and leave to prove. When doubled in size knead again.
Divide and mould into loaves, putting the dough into well-
greased tins. When the dough has risen again, place loaves in
oven heat just above 300 F and **bake** for one hour. Turn out
loaves onto a wire tray.

KORNKNACKER BREAD

From Miss Juliet Vingoe, Horse and Jockey Bakery, Helston

This unusual bread has been baked in Helston since September 1989 and is proved in baskets to give the attractive basket-weave imprint on the finished loaf. The kornknacker concentrate is bought from Holgran, a subsidiary of Rank Hovis McDougall, based in Burton-on-Trent.

Ingredients

4 lbs (2 kg) Kornknacker concentrate (wheat flour, coarse rye meal, diced soya, sunflower seeds, linseed, sesame seeds, dried sour dough, soyabran, malt flour, aniseed and caraway seeds, salt)

4lbs (2 kg) white flour

5 oz (120 g) yeast

5 lbs (2.400 kg) water

Method Mix all ingredients for 2 minutes on first speed in spiral mixer and then for 6 minutes on second speed. Rest in bulk for 30 minutes. Knock back and scale into 460 g loaves. Mould rounds and place in tins or baskets on a tray. Prove for 50-60 minutes.

Bake at 450 F for 20-30 minutes.

WHITE VIENNA CRUSTIES

As made by Mr Arthur Tonkin, Cresta Bakery, Helston

Ingredients
70 lbs (31.750 kg) white flour
$1^{1}/_{4}$ lbs (560 g) salt
$1^{1}/_{4}$ lbs (560 g) commercial bread improver
2 lbs (900 g) fresh yeast
18 quarts (20 litres) water at 80°

Method Mix to a dough and then place in vertical mixer and mix on a faster speed for 15 minutes to develop the dough. Weigh off into 4 oz portions or weights, doing this quickly to prevent excessive rising. Prove for 20 minutes.
Bake for 20-30 minutes at 425-450 F.

CHINESE BREAD

From Mr Keith Willey, Mullion Bakery

This is a strange-looking round white loaf, with small, spiky raised squares on top. Mullion bakery have been making Chinese bread for the past three years and it was introduced by a bakery worker from Camborne. A similarly shaped loaf, called a hedgehog, is sold at Boscastle Bakery in the north of the county.

Ingredients
70 lbs (31.750 kg) untreated strong white bread flour
1 lb 2 oz (510 g) salt
1 lb (450 g) white shortening
2 oz (50 g) sugar
1 block yeast (2 lb 3 oz) (1 kg)
40 lbs water (18 litres) (the exact quantity usually guessed)
Yield: 110 x 1lb loaves

Method Mix dough for 25 minutes in conventional mixer and leave to rest for 40 minutes. Knock back and leave to rest for a further 10 minutes. Scale, mould into round cob shapes and prove for 25 minutes. Before the final proving, cut the dough with a sharp knife, making a chequer-board effect on the top of the loaf.

Bake at 440 F for 45 minutes.

SOFT GRANARY ROLLS

From Mr Malcolm Gilbert, St Keverne Bakery

Baking from his own, modern industrial unit on the outskirts of St Keverne, Mr Malcolm Gilbert combines the advantages of modern baking technology with a village bakery in a rural setting. He bakes two varieties of granary rolls, crusty and soft but finds that the softer rolls are more popular.

Ingredients

4 lbs (1.8 kg) Granary flour
1 lb (450 g) white flour
$1^1/_2$ oz (40 g) salt
$^1/_2$ oz (15 g) sugar
1 oz (25 g) additives and preservatives
6 oz (160 g) lard
4 oz (110 g) yeast
Approx. $2^1/_2$ pints (1.4 litres) water
The quantities given are sufficient for four dozen rolls.

Method Mix dry ingredients together and then add the yeast with a little water. Add remaining water to obtain the correct consistency. Mix in large mixer until smooth, about 2-3 minutes. Place on table and leave dough until it 'moves'. Weigh up into 3 oz rolls. Tray up and place in prover for about $^1/_2$ hour.

Bake for 15 minutes at 450 F.

FALMOUTH

WITH the influx of holiday makers during the summer months, bread (and pasties) sell well in Falmouth. Choak's put their pasty making on show in the bakery window in Killigrew Street and it proves quite a tourist attraction. They used to sell the Dutch slimming loaf, Malsovit; a diet bread made with bran, whole wheat, barley and a variety of other flours; but it was never popular with customers and has been discontinued. The advantage was that it kept well and the slices were satisfying but it was expensive: over £2.50 a loaf. Mr Choak gives the recipe for a *Hovis loaf*, again no longer made but the bread is still well advertised within the shop.

Sadly, a newcomer to the area, Mr Terry Satchwill at Terry's Bakery in Arwenack Street, has recently closed his business. He had been baking for the past thirty years, mostly in the south of England, but also in the United States. But whilst in Falmouth, he introduced several unusual and popular loaves into his bread shop and café, Lincoln plum bread and a *cinnamon bread*, for example. He had intended to modernize the twenty-five year old gas-fired bakery ovens that he had inherited from Mr G. Hooper, who retired in 1990. A recipe by Mr Hooper before his retirement, for an *organic loaf* is given. Terry Satchwill also baked a wholemeal organic loaf, obtaining his organic flour from Harbertonford Watermill, near Totnes, Devon, the closest mill to Cornwall. The gap in the market has now been taken over by Choak's in Killigrew Street who supply their organic bread to the local health shops.

W.C. Rowe's Bakery, based in Penryn, has many selling outlets in the area. It is basically a family firm which has expanded into a small factory, selling bread, rolls and cakes to shops in Falmouth and the surrounding villages, and increasingly to supermarkets.

Rolls of all shapes and varieties seem to sell well in

Falmouth; they are ideal for holiday makers wanting a change from pasties for their picnic lunches in the summer. Rowe's sell French and Vienna crusty rolls in white flour and rustic crusties in brown — they look rather like batons or short French sticks. According to Mr Roger Day at Rowe's bakery, the *rustic French crusties* are one of their most popular lines and in the summer they bake as many as four thousand overnight. Another type of brown roll, a hoagy, has recently been marketed, but as yet acceptance has been limited. Always ready to expand their range of bread and tempt the market, Rowe's have recently introduced a choice grain bread, made with 'combicorn' concentrate and incorporating a wide variety of different grains.

Batches in Falmouth are round and crusty and sandwich loaves are known as underpans. The round barrel-shaped milk loaf is appropriately called a concertina.

RUSTIC FRENCH CRUSTIES

From Mr Roger Day at Rowe's Bakery, Penryn

The quantities given are in so-called 'bakers' terms'.

Ingredients

70% unbleached untreated wholewheat flour
30% unbleached untreated wholewheat flakes
60% or 60 parts water
3% yeast
2% salt
10% rustic improver

Method All-in-one method. The ingredients are mixed together for 10 minutes in the spiral mixer, semi-fast speed. The dough is then divided into 3oz weights for each roll and left to prove for an hour.

Bake in hot oven for 25 minutes, with a steam injection at the start of baking, to produce the crispy crust.

HOVIS RECIPE

From Mr Charlie Choak, of J. H. and M. Choak, Falmouth

An old-fashioned loaf favoured by older customers.

The name 'Hovis' has been in existence for the past hundred years, since 1890, when a £25 prize was awarded to Herbert Grime, a student winning the competition for a suitable name. Hovis is a foreshortening of *hominis vis*, meaning the strength of man. Since then, the Hovis range has expanded considerably and now boasts eleven different varieties, with such loaves as Hovis Country Grain, Stone-ground, Hovis Mildbake and even a Hovis white.

Ingredients

4 lb (1.8 kg) Hovis flour. As the Hovis flour contains salt, no extra salt needs to be added.

1 oz (25 g) fat

3 oz (75 g) fresh yeast

2 pints (1.1 litre) water

The above ingredients are sufficient for six loaves.

Method All the ingredients are added together and then mixed for 4 minutes in a conventional mixer. The resulting dough is then weighed off into 480 g pieces (when these are baked, a 400 g loaf is produced). After proving, the loaves are baked at 240 C for 35 minutes.

CINNAMON BREAD

From Mr Terry Satchwill, Terry's Bakery

Unusually, the dough is chopped into small pieces before being placed into the tin for the final proving. The finished loaf has an attractive dark, spiky crust, giving a chunky appearance.

Ingredients

3 lbs (1.35 kg) white flour

$^1/_2$ lb (225 g) white sugar

$^1/_2$ lb (225 g) margarine

28oz (700ml) warm water

3oz (75 g) yeast

Method Mix for 10 minutes on low speed, then let the dough rest for 30 minutes. Pin the dough out and add:

4 eggs

$^1/_2$ oz (15 g) cinnamon

$^1/_2$ oz (15 g) mixed spice

8 oz (225 g) demerara sugar

Blend the above ingredients into the dough by hand and then chop into small pieces. Weigh into greased and floured tins at 1 lb weight. Prove until the dough reaches the top of the tin.

Bake at 400 F for 20-25 minutes.

ORGANIC LOAF

From Mr George Hooper, Falmouth

Ingredients
$3^1/_2$ lbs (1.575 kg) organic Dove Farm flour
1 oz (25 g) salt
1 oz (25 g) malt extract
$1^1/_4$ oz (35 g) yeast
2 pints (1.1 litre) water
The above quantities are sufficient for three large loaves.

Method Mix dry ingredients together and add water. Leave to rise for $^1/_2$ hour, knock back and then leave for a further half an hour. Scale off into 1 lb and 2 lb loaves and leave to rise for half an hour. Before baking, sprinkle the loaves with wheat flakes.

Bake at 480 F for 30 minutes for small loaves and 40 minutes for large loaves.

TRURO

CONSIDERING that Truro is so well endowed with retail shops, it is surprising that the town has no resident small bakers. Mrs Allen at Tina's Celebration Cake Shop in River Street has recently started to offer her customers a small selection of bread and rolls, but her main interest is in confectionery. The larger bakery chains are well represented, with Blewett's (now a branch of W.T. Warren) and W.C. Rowe's from Penryn, as well as Tesco's with their in-store bakery. Here customers can park with ease and choose from a wide selection of bread. Most of the bread is based on the same *white bread* recipe; the dough is moulded into different shapes and sizes and sometimes covered with seeds for variety. The names are dictated by national guidelines, with few local variations. Other bread is bought in from the larger bakeries and Hovis, for example, can be bought in a variety of forms.

The only really small baker in Truro is Mr Way from Grampound and his recipe for *Granary Bread* is given. He has a popular outlet in the indoor market and queues form early here for his hot and inexpensive pasties. When Mr Way's father began baking in the area, in 1935, there were six other bakeries nearby; now Mr Way is the sole survivor. He has seen many changes; more brown bread is being sold, but white is still more popular with his customers and over the years the sales of bread have declined in favour of cakes — a real sign of the times. The bakery has a retail sales van, visiting individual customers, which is unusual nowadays, as well as a shop in the market in Falmouth.

South of Truro, Mr Chesterman runs the Devoran Bakery from an industrial unit in Falmouth. He comes from the West Midlands and his names are national rather than regional. The bakery supplies bread to retailers in the surrounding area and as sales are largely targeted at the resident population, they are less affected by fluctuations in the summer tourist trade.

WHITE BREAD – BASIC DOUGH

From Mr L. Gale, manager at Tesco's In-store Bakery, Truro

This dough is used as the base for most of the bread sold in the store. The size and shape of the loaves can be varied and the final dough can be dipped into maw or sesame seeds before baking to give variety.

Ingredients

70 lbs (32 kg) white flour

$2^1/_2$ lbs (1.2 kg) bread concentrate

2 lb (1 kg) yeast

4 gallons (18 litres) water (litres and kilogrammes weigh the same)

Method Mix for 3 minutes in high speed mixer. Process into 2 lb (960 g) or 1 lb (480 g) weights. Mould and dip into sesame or maw seeds before baking at 425 F for 35 minutes.

GRANARY BREAD

From Mr Derek Way, Grampound

This is Mr Way's favourite loaf.

Ingredients

$3^1/_2$ lbs (1.575 kg) granary flour

1 oz (25 g) salt

$^1/_2$ oz (15 g) fat

$^1/_4$ oz (10 g) improver

$1^3/_4$ oz (45 g) yeast

$^1/_2$ lb or 32 fluid oz (450 g) water

Method Mix for 8 minutes in spiral mixer: 2 minutes slow and 6 minutes fast. Weigh off into 1 lb (400 g) loaves, mould by hand and prove for 45-50 minutes.

Bake at 450 F for 25-30 minutes.

PERRANPORTH

PERRANPORTH is dominated by the tourists, who flock into St Piran's Parade during the summer months. The bakeries in the main street just manage to survive in the winter but they have difficulty in keeping up with the demand for bread during the holiday season.

Baking starts early and the tourists call soon after 5.30 am to collect their breakfast bread and rolls. Indeed, an early morning walk to the bakery is one of the holiday highlights for many people. Perhaps the Cornwall Tourist Board should promote this as one of the attractions of the area?

Mr Farnfield at the Homemade Bakery baked several unusual breads; sadly, he has recently ceased trading. Particularly attractive was his *Cheese and Onion Bread*, a long bloomer-shaped loaf covered in melted cheese. Crusty's offer garlic bread, as well as cheese and bacon rolls and Rippons Bakery has been a family business for the past fifty years and is popular with both local residents and tourists.

Names for the bread are fairly standard, although tin loaves can come as tall tins, round tins and three-quarter tins as well as the usual small tins. Batches are round and milk loaves are known as small rings.

CHEESE AND ONION BREAD

From Mr Farnfield, formerly at The Homemade Bakery

The loaf is made from a basic white bread dough, with added onions, and then it is scattered with grated cheese before baking. As the bread bakes, the cheese soaks into the loaf, giving a strongly-flavoured cheesy taste. Unfortunately, quantities were not given.

Ingredients
White bread flour (treated)
Salt
Fat
Fresh yeast
Water
Processed or dried onions

Method Weigh in all ingredients (except onions). Mix for 20-25 minutes on a conventional mixer. Add onions five minutes before the end of the mixing time. Allow to prove for 25 minutes. Knock back. Form into bloomer-shape loaves, prove for 45 minutes. Egg wash and sprinkle with grated cheese.

Bake for 30-45 minutes depending on the volume being baked. Temperature 450 F.

This loaf is supposed to be a soft loaf with a shelf life of three days. Can also be warmed up and eaten hot.

NEWQUAY

TOURISTS coming to Newquay are well served with bakeries. There are two traditional businesses, Ellery's and the Edgcumbe Bakery and two more recent establishments, The Bread Basket and Jamie's Patisserie, run by a member of the Barnecutt baking family.

At The Bread Basket you can buy thick chunky, crusty rolls called *torpedoes* while at Ellery's Bakery smaller, white, soft boat-shaped rolls are known as eggs. Here, Mr Ellery has a wide selection of bread on show, with a café alongside and bakery behind. He believes that many of the old-fashioned methods and recipes are best and he still uses the long fermentation time for proving, for example, his *sour dough*. Along the walls of the café he displays harvest plaques and shields, made with bread dough and then varnished. Rye bread and Vit B. are made weekly at Ellery's. The Edgcumbe Bakery occasionally bake a crown loaf, a circular wholemeal bread, cut into four and sprinkled with cracked wheat.

A new name for the large tin loaf emerges in Newquay, where it is called a round top. Sandwich loaves are underpans and you can even buy a square underpan and a long underpan.

TORPEDOES

From Mr Ted Burns, The Bread Basket, Newquay

These short rolls are made with the dough for French sticks which is then cut into three before baking.

Ingredients

70 lb (32 kg) of untreated special fail-safe white flour.

4 gallons (19 litres) water

4$^{1}/_{2}$ lb (2 kg) yeast

5$^{1}/_{2}$ lb (2.5 kg) British Arkady Bronze concentrate

Method No time dough. Mix on high speed for 3 minutes. Place on table and cut into 12 oz dough pieces. Mould and rest and put dough onto French stick wires. Make 7 shallow cuts along the top and cut dough into three. Long prove — for 45 minutes.

Bake at 271 C or 500 F, steaming until the temperature drops to 180 C, 220 F, baking altogether for 15-20 minutes.

SOUR DOUGH

Two recipes from Mr Chris Ellery's Bakery, Newquay

This dough is used for a variety of bread: tins, bloomers, farmhouse and cottage loaves.

Ingredients
70 lbs (31.8 kg) untreated strong white baker's flour
$1^1/_4$ lbs (570 g) salt
$1^1/_2$ lbs (680 g) fresh yeast
4 oz (100 g) sugar (to give bloom on the crust)

Method The dough is knocked up in the afternoon and mixed to a slacker than usual consistency with about 2 gallons of warm water. The dough is then left in the mixer until the next morning, when the following ingredients are added:
70 lbs (31.8 kg) white flour
$1^1/_2$ lbs (680 g) salt
$2^1/_4$ lb (1 kg) yeast
$1^1/_4$ lb (570 g) lard
$2^1/_4$ gallons (11.4 litres) warm water — depending on the flour absorption

The dough is mixed until it comes off the mixer in a tight dough and is then left in the mixer for $1^1/_2$ hours. Scale and mould roughly and leave for a further 20-30 minutes. Make up into final loaf shapes — tins, bloomers, etc. Final proving $^3/_4$ hour.

Bake at 490 F with a falling heat; the oven is switched off and the bread cooks for 35 minutes. This is possible because Mr Ellery uses the old-fashioned bakery oven with thick walls which retain heat well. Peels are still used to remove the bread from the oven.

VIENNA LOAF

A long, thin bloomer, with cuts on top, decorated with poppy or sesame seeds. Mr Ellery usually adds a piece of dough from a richer dough to the Vienna loaf ingredients.

Ingredients
14 lbs (6.4 kg) flour
6 oz (170 g) yeast
3 oz (85 g) salt
5$\frac{1}{4}$ pints (3 litres) warm water
2 eggs

Method Straight mix, scale into 1 lb or 2 lb weights (500 g or 1 kg weights). Mould roughly and roll into shape. Leave for half an hour. Mould into final shape and prove for a further $\frac{3}{4}$ hour. Coat with egg wash and decorate with poppy or sesame seeds before baking.

Bake for 20-25 minutes at 425 F.

INDIAN QUEENS

IT is sad to see the demise of one of the most original and enthusiastic bakers in the county. Until 1991, Mr Small baked from one of the small industrial units at the rear of the old school in Indian Queens. The bread was then sold from his nearby shop and café in St Columb Minor as well as to other retail shops, hotels and public houses in the area. A real enthusiast for his trade and willing to experiment with new shapes and ingredients, Mr Small's bakery deserved recommendation — hedgehogs, tortoises and harvest plaques were made regularly, and many of these were coated with resin and sold for display.

In the China Clay District, St Dennis and Nanpean have their own small bakeries. Hendra Bakery at St Dennis was established almost a hundred years ago and must rank as one of the oldest bakeries in Cornwall. A photograph shows the bakery as it was over fifty years ago and to all outward appearances it has changed very little since then. The present owners, Mr and Mrs John Rowe, have been in St Dennis for the past fifteen years and they have other retail bread shops at St Stephens and Roche. In addition, Mr Rowe goes out on a house-to-house delivery van service three times a week. Both granary and malt crunch loaves are baked at St Dennis, large split tin loaves are called farmhouse and the ordinary brown loaves are known as large or small meals. One unusual line is a yeast seed loaf and coming from Warren's at St Just, Mr Rowe bakes kettle and mansion loaves, cottage and harvest loaves to special order.

Mr and Mrs Sherrif run the W.A. French and Son Bakery at Nanpean. Good, wholesome bread is on offer and there is a delicious smell of freshly-baked bread as one enters the shop. However, they must suffer from competition from the nearby supermarkets in St Austell with the lower prices and wider choice of bread. Unfortunately, the long-established bakery at Bugle has now closed down, depriving the community of its own village bakery.

OAT AND RAISIN LOAF

From Mr Small, Indian Queens

The ingredients are particularly suitable for anyone looking for a low calorie, low cholesterol diet.

Ingredients

7 oz (200 g) white or untreated flour
7 oz (200 g) wholemeal flour
1 oz (25 g) baking powder
Pinch of salt
$^1/_2$ oz (15 g) cinnamon
$^1/_2$ oz (15 g) nutmeg
5 oz (135 g) rolled oats
8 oz (225 g) demerara sugar
14 fluid oz (third of litre) water
$1^1/_2$ oz (40 g) milk powder
3 eggs or 5 oz in weight
2 fluid oz (50 ml) cooking oil (sunflower or other vegetable oil)
8 oz (225 g) raisins or sultanas
The quantities make 2 **x** 1lb loaves.

Method All in one. Stir together, weigh off into 1 lb pieces, place in greased loaf tin, taking care to grease with vegetable fat.

Bake in slow oven, 340 F or 170 C for 45 mins-1 hour, until set. Turn out and cool on tray. Best eaten 2-3 days later.

ROSELAND

THE small number of bakers on the Roseland reflects the problem of serving a scattered rural community. There are few large shops in the area and just two small bakeries, at St Mawes and Portscatho.

At St Mawes, Mr Patrick Curtis runs a small, family bakery, behind the main street. He supplies a shop and snack bar in St Mawes, together with a few other shops and hotels in the area. Demand for his bread of course is far greater during the summer months and then he employs another bakery worker, making a total workforce of just three. At Portscatho, Greg's Bakery has only been open for about two years, and his bread is for sale in the local store.

Names on the Roseland are very standard, with a large white or crusty, sandwich or underpan. The only real variation is a Danish loaf baked by Mr Curtis — a short, bloomer-shaped loaf with cuts across, known as a batch in parts of East Cornwall.

ST AUSTELL

SURPRISINGLY, most of the recipes from the St Austell area are for fruit loaves. Perhaps the residents here have a taste and predilection for sweet bread? With an abundance of small, thriving bakeries as well as competition from the larger supermarkets, the bread-buying public have plenty of choice. Some bakers are reluctant to disclose the ingredients for their saffron loaves, but in St Austell I was given the recipes quite freely. Perhaps the area can be called the home of the *saffron loaf*, especially as the large saffron bun, a Cornish tea treat in the rest of the county, is called a *feast bun* in St Austell. Even Noel Coward, the playwright, when visiting Charlestown in 1914, remembers saffron cake as being 'bright yellow and delicious'.

Names for bread are disappointingly routine, with the large tin loaf being called a long or short split or alternatively a large or small crusty. Then sandwich loaves are known as underpans. The names Danish, batch and bloomer are used for a variety of shapes and sizes and the traditional cottage loaf is baked regularly. Bakeries in other areas tend to fight shy of this loaf, which is labour intensive and expensive to produce.

In St Austell town, there are four small bakers, the delightfully old-fashioned Greenaways Bakery, with their forty-year-old coke-fired ovens, the bustling, up-to-date Fresh N Crusty Hot Bread Shop in Vicarage Place, as well as Martin's and Nile's. The Niles have been part of the St Austell baking scene for over thirty years and they have several shops in the area; Mr and Mrs M.A. Hawkin have been running Martin's Bakery in Clifden Road for the past twelve years. The position of their shop, on the outskirts of the town and in a no-parking area, sadly must restrict their trade, although they have another shop in the popular holiday resort of Mevagissey.

Outside St Austell, Mrs Lewis sells from the Crusty Loaf at Mevagissey, there is the Cakebread Bakery at Gorran Haven and Par Bakery is run by Mr and Mrs P. Wild. At the Cakebread Bakery, I noticed a strange-looking dumpy loaf, apparently baked for the proprietor from the left-over dough at the end of the day — an interesting idea.

Within St Austell, special mention should be made of the impressive range of bread available from the in-store bakery at Asda, run by Mr Brimble. Although not particularly Cornish, customers can buy a full range of continental breads, with such intriguing names as daktyla, hellesroggenbrot, dunkelroggenbrot, veneziani, bocconcini, vielsaatbrot, or rustikall. Also on offer are multi grain and rye loaves, bornhoffen and rye loaves, onion and rye, as well as cheddar cheese bread. The latter is so popular that the bakery have difficulty in keeping up with demand. To Asda's credit, their large white split tin loaf received a commendation from the BBC's Food and Drink programme recently — 'it's wonderful'.

Recipes from the area include tiger topping from Martin's Bakery — in other areas the ingredients for this recipe are a closely-guarded secret. Then there is the feast bun from Niles, the saffron loaf from Mr Greenaway, a traditional *bun loaf* from the Fresh N Crusty Hot Bread shop and fruit and nut bread from Par Bakery.

TRADITIONAL BUN LOAF

From Mr Ray Ball at the Fresh N Crusty Hot Bread Shop, St Austell

The final glazing gives a special dark and shiny top to the loaf.

Ingredients

$3^{1}/_{4}$ lb (1.6 kg) bakers' flour
1 oz (20 g) salt
4 oz (100 g) sugar
4 oz (100 g) white shortening
4 oz (100 g) yeast
Approx. 2 lb (900) g water
7 oz (200 g) sultanas
10 oz (300 g) currants

Method Mixing time depends on the style of the mixer. High speed 3 mins, standard 25 mins. Rest for 40 mins, then add fruit on slow speed. Rest 15 mins, then scale out, large 600 g or small 370 g. Prove until level with top of tin, for approx. 30 minutes.

Bake at 450 F for 15 mins until the sides are brown.

Glaze with sugar and water as soon as the loaf is taken out of the oven; the heat caramelizes the sugar.

SAFFRON LOAF

From Mr Stanley Greenaway, Greenaways, St Austell

Ingredients
$2^1/_2$ lb (1.12 kg) strong plain white flour
8 oz (225 g) sugar
9 oz (250 g) lard. (At Christmas Mr Greenaway uses butter
  instead of lard.)
1 lb (450 g) currants
2 oz (50 g) peel
Pinch saffron (5 g)
3 oz (75 g) yeast
3 eggs
$^1/_2$ pint (260 ml) water
Quantities for 3 large loaves
Method Soak the saffron overnight in some of the water. Put
flour in bowl with sugar and lard and mix to a crumbly mess.
Then ferment yeast with a quarter of a pint of water for a
short time and small fermentation. Put into dough hook
machine with the eggs. Add saffron (and water) with the
remaining water. Mix until clear and add fruit. Prove in the
machine for 30 minutes. Scale off into 14 oz weights. Prove
in the tin until the dough reaches to almost the top of the tin,
about half an hour.
Bake at 400 F for 35 minutes.

FEAST BUNS

From Mr John Nile, at Leslie Nile's Bakery, St Austell

These buns are a regular and popular line especially with Sunday School parties.

Ingredients

3 lbs (1.350 kg) strong plain white flour

$^1/_4$ oz (10 g) salt

6 oz (170 g) sugar

1 lb (450 g) lard

3 oz (75 g) yeast

$1^1/_4$ lb (675 g) currants

Saffron, about 20 grains, soaked overnight with some of the water

Approx. 16-20 oz water

Method Mix yeast and a little sugar with some of the warm water, leave to ferment for 20 minutes. Rub fat into flour and mix in the remaining water, yeast mixture and saffron. Work in the dough hook machine for 2-3 minutes and then add currants. Prove 30 minutes. Scale off into 6 oz weights, mould into bun shapes by hand and leave to prove for a further 30 minutes until the required size is reached.

Bake at 400 F for 15 minutes.

TIGER TOPPING

From Mr Martin Hawkin of Martin's Bakery, St Austell

The topping is spread over any white loaf just before the final proving. The finished loaf has a rich and flaky topping, definitely enhancing the flavour.

Ingredients

10 oz (275 g) oil

40 oz (1.120 ml) water

3 lb (1.35 kg) rice cones (this is rather like ground rice and is not so finely milled as flour)

Method Mix ingredients together until a soft dropping consistency is reached. Spread by hand over about 25 loaves.
Bake at 420 F for 30 minutes.

FRUIT AND NUT BREAD

From Mrs Sue Wild, Par Bakery

An attractive pale yellow loaf, with the cherries, nuts and peel giving colour.

Ingredients

2 lb (900 g) plain cake flour
1 oz (25 g) baking powder
1$^{1}/_{4}$ lb (560g) granulated sugar
8 oz (225 g) lard
8 oz (225 g) margarine or butter
1 lb (450 g) eggs
1 oz (25 g) milk powder
9 oz (250 g) sultanas
9 oz (250 g) currants
2 oz (50 g) mixed peel
2 oz (50 g) cherries
10 oz (275 g) water
Vanilla and almond essence

Method Cream sugar and fat. Add eggs and flour and then baking powder and milk powder. Mix in the currants and dried fruit, followed by the water and essences. Scatter with flaked almonds before **baking** in a 14 oz loaf tin at just below 180 C, depending on the oven, for approximately 45-50 minutes.

LOSTWITHIEL AND BODMIN

ALTHOUGH geographically close, in terms of bread, Bodmin and Lostwithiel are worlds apart. Bodmin is the home of the Malcolm Barnecutt chain of bakery stores, with their large, highly organized and mechanized bakery on the Carminow Industrial estate. Lostwithiel, in contrast, proudly boasts a really traditional cottage bakery, tucked away in a side street at the back of the town, away from the main traffic thoroughfare.

Although Malcolm Barnecutt has been baking independently since 1983, he still uses many of the well tried recipes, from the original family firm in Wadebridge. Another member of the Barnecutt family, Jamie Barnecutt, has recently started baking in Newquay.

Much of the white bread in Bodmin is baked with unbleached and untreated flour and unusually granary bread is baked in an undertin or sandwich loaf shape. One recent introduction is herb bread. The mix is bought in from Abel and Schafer, a German firm based in Southampton, and twelve different herbs are mixed in with a blend of grains. To quote from the firm's promotional literature, 'A blend of several grains, seeds and twelve selected herbs known for their medicinal qualities. This hearty bread is low in calories and has a truly unique taste. Only unbleached and unbromated flours are used — no shortening or sugar added'. The herbs are clubmoss, nettle leaves, coriander, camomile, parsley, balm leaves, dutch rush, bean kraut, hawthorn leaves, basil, dill and mint.

The Lostwithiel Bakery is one of a selected handful of bakers in Cornwall to make bread for the Everlasting Bakery, from Launceston. This imaginative small firm treat the loaves with preservative and varnish to retain the shape and colour, looking as good as new, year after year. The bread is then sold for display in restaurants, bakery shops or to individuals who want an attractive and unusual ornament.

Mr Jim Wheeler runs the Lostwithiel Bakery and he offers his customers some unusual and speciality lines: harvest loaves, plaits, rolls in the shape of mice, and even a plaited bloomer — a normal bloomer loaf with an attractive long plait along the top. Pasties are sold with a variety of ingredients, and they are then dusted with different toppings: vegetarian pasties are covered with chopped parsley, cheese and onion pasties have parsley on one half and the traditional pasties are kept plain. A unique product is the boat loaf, shaped rather like a Coburg loaf but more oval in shape. It is made with rye flour, slashed across the crust and then dusted with a mixture of sesame and sunflower seeds — deliciously soft and fresh to eat.

HERB BREAD

From Abel and Schafer Ltd., Southampton

Ingredients
10 kg (21$\frac{1}{4}$ lbs) Herb Bread Mix
6-6.5 kg (13 lbs) Water
0.2 kg (7 oz) Yeast
Batch weight 16.700 kg (35$\frac{1}{2}$ lbs)
Method Ferment yeast 30-40 mins. Knead dough mixture with spiral kneader, 5 mins. on 1st speed, 8-10 mins 2nd speed, elevating kneader; 15 mins slowly, 15 mins. fast. Scale 450g (1 lb) to give long or round shape. Put in baskets or moulds for proving. Prove 45-60 mins., with dough temp at 25-27 C. Start baking with steam, then pull damper. **Bake** at approx. 250 C to start, 200 C to finish, for 45-55 mins., according to bread weight.

PADSTOW

PADSTOW is well known for its harbour, the hobby 'oss and the tourists who crowd into the narrow confines and streets of the town during the summer months. Prideaux Place hosts many visitors, but another attraction should be Padstow's own home bakery, one of several bakers' shops in the town.

The Cornerhouse Bakery in Lanadwell Street, run by Mr and Mrs M.J. Howells, displays an attractive range of bread. Here, visitors can buy the Cornish crown loaf, a type of farl bread, baked with wholemeal flour and cut into four before baking. If customers are feeling particularly economical, they can buy just one section at a time and this is much appreciated by pensioners. Rounds are attractive round loaves with soft sides and dusted with a mixture of seeds and cracked wheat. Then there are larger than average bloomers, in white, wholemeal or granary, which when displayed alongside the rounds, crown loaves, cobs and long tin loaves give the shop a wholesome, old-fashioned aura. Splits are not made by the bakery; according to Mr Howells, the visitors prefer to eat the sweeter scones with their cream teas.

CROWN LOAF

From Mr M. Howells, Cornerhouse Bakery, Padstow

A distinctive-looking loaf, in four sections, and only baked by a few bakeries in the county.

Ingredients

$3^{1}/_{2}$ lb (1.575 kg) good quality stoneground wholemeal flour

Dash of orange juice or small quantity of Vitamin C. Improvers are now permitted with wholemeal flour and they help the bread to rise and then hold its shape. This is particularly critical when the dough is moved from the prover at the final stage and into the oven.

2 oz (50 g) lard or bread fat — gives the loaf keeping quality

2 oz (50 g) fresh yeast. If dried yeast is used, this should be sprinkled on top of the ingredients at the start of mixing. With home baking, generally more yeast is needed than in the bakery.

Small handful of cracked or stippled wheat

2 oz (50 g) dark brown sugar — this gives the bread a nutty taste and helps the yeast to rise.

2 oz (50 g) salt — this is important, again to help the bread rise. $1^{3}/_{4}$-2 pints water — with stoneground flour, use plenty of water to make a spongy dough. In the summer, cold water can be used.

Method Dissolve yeast in a small quantity of water, adding a little sugar. Mix all ingredients in a spiral mixer for 20 minutes. At home, use a mixer with a dough hook, if available. Otherwise blend thoroughly, rubbing fat into the flour and kneading mixture well.

Shape mixture into 1 lb or 2 lb balls, cover and leave for 10 minutes.

Moisten top of balls with water or weak brine, dredge with flour and cut each ball into four with a palette knife, making sure that the cuts go right to the bottom of the dough. Prove again in a warm place for about an hour, depending on the heat of the kitchen. **Bake** at Gas 7 or 450-470 F for about $^{3}/_{4}$ hour. The timing depends on the oven; a full oven requires the full time. Usually at home, there is less in the oven and so a lower heat and shorter time can be used.

WADEBRIDGE AND ROCK

Two enthusiastic bakers serve this area: Mr Michael Jenkins, who runs the Keith Barnecutt bakery in Wadebridge and Mrs Rita Masters in Rock. Both bakeries are very different. Rock Bakery is run as a small family business whereas Barnecutt's is a larger commercial undertaking. Both areas have a generous tourist trade in the summer with quiet winter trading months. Barnecutt's tend to maintain their custom throughout the year, however, with wholesale sales to public houses as well as to retail shops in Wadebridge, Newquay, Padstow and St Columb Major.

Mr Jenkins' enthusiasm for his profession is infectious, as he speaks about the pleasure of coming to work each morning and seeing row upon row of newly-baked bread. The sight and smell never fail to lift his spirits. Following the death of Mr Keith Barnecutt, Mr Jenkins took over this branch of the Barnecutt bakery in 1988 and he has worked for the firm now for over thirty years.

The split tin loaf at Barnecutt's is rather unusual because Mr Jenkins always cuts his loaves to the bottom of the dough before baking, giving a higher loaf with a wider bloom. Batches are round, sandwich loaves are undertins and a milk loaf is known as a fluted, with a further variation giving a fluted bun loaf. Mr Jenkins has provided me with a recipe for an unusual *malt loaf*.

In nearby Rock, Mrs Rita Masters and her daughter run the village bakery. Mrs Masters concentrates on the bread and bakery side of the business, whereas her daughter specializes in confectionery. There has been a bakery in Rock for over sixty years and during this time it has been expanded and improved. The original coal-fired ovens have been replaced by modern electric ovens and although some of the old bread troughs are still *in situ*, they are now used as work tops. Mrs Masters has been in the bakery since she left school and learnt her trade from an older employee, well qualified as a master baker.

Bloomers in Rock are made in white, brown or wholemeal as well as in harvester flour. Sandwich loaves are undertins and a brown stick is a soft baguette type of loaf. As a variation on saffron buns, you can even buy saffron tea cakes. Mrs Masters gives a proprietary recipe for a *muesli loaf* and I could not resist a recipe for rock buns from Rock bakery.

MALT LOAF

From Mr Michael Jenkins, the Keith Barnecutt Bakery, Wadebridge

This is not one of Mr Jenkins' regular lines, but he makes it now and again when he feels like adding some variety to his bread output.

Ingredients

1¹/₂ lb (675 g) Malt flour (this is light brown in colour and contains all the concentrates for making malt bread)

To this is added:

2¹/₂ lbs (1.125 kg) Bread flour (white)

1¹/₂ oz (40 g) yeast

2 lbs (900 g) water

³/₄ lb (275 g) sultanas

Method Add yeast to water and then mix into flour. Allow to prove for 90 mins. Knock back and scale into 10¹/₂-oz-size loaves. Place in tins and prove, covered with a sheet of plastic, until the dough reaches the top of the tin. Place a baking tray over the dough for about 5 mins. and when the dough touches this surface, remove the trays and slide the loaves into the oven.

Bake at about 380 F for 45 mins.

Mr Jenkins has very definite ideas about proving. The liquid should always be colder than the room temperature and should be allowed to rise to the temperature in the atmosphere. He covers the dough with new dustbin liners as plastic covers and he says that you can feel the warmth from the dough under the covers. In the summer, the bakery is so hot that he uses cold water for making bread and the dough absorbs the heat and warmth from the atmosphere.

MUESLI LOAF

From Mrs Rita Masters, Rock Bakery

Ingredients
2 lb (900 g) muesli (this is a special mix from Edme flour merchants and contains nuts and flakes, but no fruit. Mrs Masters sometimes adds her own fruit to the mix and believes that she is the only bakery in the area making this loaf)

To this is added:

2 lb (900 g) flour (brown)

$^1/_2$ oz (15 g) salt

1 quart (1.1 litre) water

4 oz (110 g) yeast

Method Add yeast to water and mix into flour. Prove for just quarter of an hour. Mould into rounds by hand and prove slightly, for barely 10 mins. Wet top of loaf and sprinkle with nuts.

Bake 400 F for 20 mins.

Mrs Masters says that this is a very quick loaf to make, just $^1/_2$ hour from the start to putting into the oven. Many holiday makers buy this in the summer and take it back home for their freezers.

German tourists during the summer and again at Christmas time. Soft rolls are called cut rounds rather than splits.

Bude has three bread shops, Headon's whose main bakery is in Holsworthy, the well established Landsdown Bakery and the more recently opened Tasty Plaice, which as its name suggests, doubles up as a café as well as a bread shop. A batch in Bude is bloomer shaped, with soft sides, the tin loaf is known as an upright and sandwich loaves are undertins or flat tops. Saffron cake is not widely made, although it is sold at the Tasty Plaice, who also market a gluten-free *rye bread* and an unusual half and half loaf. This is baked in the shape of a small tin loaf, with one half in white dough and the other half in brown and is ideal for families where some members ask for white bread and the others prefer brown. In general, bakers fight shy of mixing different doughs; the proving and baking times are difficult to regulate and the brown bread tends to go stale more quickly than the white.

RYE BREAD

From Mr Ian Biddlecombe of The Tasty Plaice, Bude

Ingredient

$3^1/_2$ lbs (1.575 kg) rye flour
$^1/_2$ oz (10 g) flour improver (soya flour)
1 oz (25 g) salt
1 oz (25 g) veg fat
2 oz (50 g) yeast
Approx. 1.75 pints (850 ml) water
Sufficient for 5 loaves

This is a quick dough; do not mix too long. The dough tends to be wet and sticky.

Method Mix for 10 mins on medium speed in Hobart mixer. Prove for 10-15 mins. in the machine. Mould and shape into 400 g bloomer-shaped loaves. Prove for 10-15 mins, until the dough splits. Spray with steam halfway through the proving time.

Bake at 220 C for about 20 mins, again spraying with water halfway through to crisp up the tops of the loaves.

ORGANIC WHOLEMEAL LOAF

From Ken's Bakery, Delabole

Ingredients

68 lbs (32 kilos) bag of organic flour
1 lb (450 g) salt
$1^1/_2$ lb (675 g) sugar
$1^1/_2$ lb (675 g) bread fat or lard
$2^1/_4$ lbs (1 kilo) block of yeast
1 bucket of water (approx 2 gallons). The amount depends on the age of the flour; the older flour is weaker and needs more water.
Sufficient for 60 x 2 lb loaves

Method Mix for 20 mins in conventional mixer (not high speed). Leave to prove for 10 mins. in mixer. Weigh out into 1 lb and 2 lb loaves and leave on the table to prove for 5-10 mins, depending on the temperature of the room. Mould by hand and then place in tins to prove for a further 20 mins. **Bake** at 450 F for 30 mins.

LINCOLN PLUM BREAD OR BARM BRACK

Two recipes from Mr Ray Clarke, Penshell Bakery, Kilkhampton

Mr Clarke bakes this bread regularly and he says that there is always a greater demand for the loaf than he can satisfy.

Ingredients
2$^{1}/_{4}$ lbs (1 kg) white flour
To which is added:
2 oz (50 g) sugar
$^{1}/_{4}$ oz (10 g) mixed spice
2 oz (50 g) fat (shortening or lard)
2 oz (50 g) yeast
Approx. 10-20 fluid oz ($^{1}/_{2}$-1 pint, $^{1}/_{4}$-$^{1}/_{2}$ litre) water
13 oz (375 g) currants
7 oz (200 g) sultanas
1$^{1}/_{2}$ oz (40 g) mixed peel

Method Mix sugar, spice and fat on Hobart mixer before adding the yeast and water. Allow to stand for half an hour, then add fruit. Scale off into 14 oz (400 g) and 16 oz (456 g) weights and mould briefly. Allow to stand for 20 mins, then re-mould and place dough in 1 lb tins. Prove until the mixture reaches the top of the tin.

Bake at 420 F for 20-30 mins, depending on the mixture. It is a rich dough and browns easily. Test by removing from the tin and tapping the base; if it sounds hollow, it is ready. Glaze with water and sugar whilst still warm.

IRISH SODA BREAD OR SODA FARL

The addition of buttermilk is traditional and bicarbonate of soda and cream of tartar are used instead of yeast as raising agents. Originating from Ireland, the bread used to be baked on open turf fires on a flat griddle, sometimes covered with an upturned pot or kettle.

Ingredients
4 lbs (1.8 kg) white flour
$^1/_2$ lb (100 g) lard
2 oz (50 g) cream of tartar
2 oz (50 g) bicarbonate of soda
1 oz (25 g) salt
$1^1/_2$ pint buttermilk

Method Mix dough and knead the mixture into a light dough. Scale off into 2 lb weights and pin out into dinner plate sizes, flatten out dough and cut each round into 4 pieces or farls. Allow to stand before **baking** at 430 F for about 20 mins.

LAUNCESTON

LAUNCESTON has several small bakeries in the centre of the town. Perhaps pride of place, though, must be given to the Southgate Bakery, attractively situated below the ancient arch, with a bow-fronted shop window, studded with bull's-eye panes. The building is dated 1884 but the bakery deeds are much older.

Terry and Maureen Parker have been running the Southgate Bakery for the past five years and make an extensive range of bread, well displayed in the shop, in baskets or along modern glass shelving. One local name to emerge is the Launceston Long John, the name given to the long tin loaf, with variations of the Long John rustic or Granary Long John. Where else but Launceston can one find Long Johns and bloomers lying side by side! Some of the breads baked by the Southgate Bakery include a seedy loaf, topped with sesame and poppy seeds, a small ridged rye loaf, a rustic wholemeal and an unusual *oatmill loaf*. The concertina or milk loaf has yet to find a name at the Southgate Bakery; customers point or call it by their own name. The batch, though, has a local touch, akin to a small tin loaf but with soft sides.

There are two bakeries in Broad Street; Malcolm Barnecutt's from Bodmin and the Launceston Bakery in the square. Here they sell two variations of the long tin loaf itself, together with a similar higher loaf, known locally as an upright. Almost opposite, in the White Hart arcade, Murphy's Bakery sells large cottage-type rolls, called crusty ploughman's rolls. It is the only bakery in the town to make the diet loaf Malsovit.

OATMILL LOAF

From Mr and Mrs Terry Parker at the Southgate Bakery, Launceston

Ingredients

7 lb (3.2 kg) oatmill flour (in the form of flakes rather than flour)

2$^{1}/_{4}$ oz (65 g) salt

1$^{1}/_{2}$ oz (45 g) sugar

1 oz (30 g) improver

2$^{1}/_{4}$ oz (65 g) vegetable fat

4 oz (115 g) yeast

Water — tepid, approx. 3 lb 12 oz (3$^{1}/_{4}$ pints or 1.8 litres)

Method

Either 1. Vertical mixer, 2 mins slow and 8 mins medium

2. Spiral mixer, 2 mins slow and 4 mins fast

3. High speed mixer, 2$^{1}/_{2}$ mins

Dough temperature — 81 F.

Scale off into 1 lb or 2 lb (400 or 800 g) weights

Prove $^{1}/_{2}$ hour.

Bake 500 F for 20-25 mins.

Batches are hand moulded but upright and tins are shaped on the mono roller.

As the old-fashioned ovens are used in the bakery, the ovens are switched off when the bread is put in; modern ovens would have to keep a constant temperature. According to Mr Parker, the dough 'sags' if it is left hanging around and so after proving, the bread should be put into the oven without delay.

CALLINGTON AREA

THERE is only one bakery in Callington, the Hot Bloomers Bakery run by Mr Doug Lewis. However, there are several other bakers in nearby villages: in both Kelly Bray and Pensilva as well as further north in Gunnislake. The area name for the large tin loaf is an *upright* or oval top and a larger version, a long tin, is also baked. A sandwich loaf is called a square or undertin.

In Callington, the Hot Bloomers Bakery has recently introduced a new rugby ball-shaped tin loaf with short cross cuts. Although it has not been given an official name in the shop, it is called a torpedo by the locals. Here, splits are no longer baked, but instead customers buy TV rolls, small triangular-shaped floured rolls which are ideal for light snacks whilst watching television — a real product of the times. *Saffron buns* are attractively displayed in an open Victorian-style basket on the shop counter. Unusually, they are not bright yellow, but pale lemon in colour, looking rather like yeast buns, but with a definite hint of saffron and deliciously light to taste.

A batch in Kelly Bray has a distinct local shape — a large white crusty oven bottom loaf with an upturned end, almost like a duck's tail. According to the proprietor, Mr Pearce, the loaf has been baked in this shape for 120 years and the recipe has been handed down through the generations. Although basically a white bread dough, the moulding by hand and special treatment gives the batch a unique flavour. In contrast, a batch in Pensilva is round and flat. Tuffs, reflecting the proximity of Devon, are made in the area rather than splits and they tend to be smaller than usual.

The delightfully situated Cottage Bakery in Gunnislake has a real flavour of nostalgia, with a small-paned bow fronted window and shelves in the shop overflowing with bread of all shapes and sizes. They sell an attractive plaited and seeded harvest ring, made with a granary type flour, as well as an unusual *rustic loaf*, round and flat and full of such healthy ingredients as cashew nuts, sunflower and sesame seeds. This recipe, from Brian O'Donnell at the Cottage Bakery, is given here.

UPRIGHT LARGE WHITE TIN LOAF

From Mr Pearce at Kelly Bray

This basic white dough can be used for other loaves of different shapes and sizes.

Ingredients

110 lbs flour (49.900 kg) — 50% untreated flour and 50% white bread flour

1¼ lbs (0.560 kg) yeast

2lb 6oz (1.1100 kg) salt

2 lb (900 g) lard or bread fat

3½ buckets (a bucket = 2 gallons) (32 litres) of water. This quantity is sufficient for 120 loaves approximately, the exact amount is judged from experience.

Method Mix in dumbrill (old fashioned dough mixer) for 15-20 mins. Then leave in the mixer to prove for 1½ hours. Take out of machine and leave in bulk to prove for a further 30-40 mins, before scaling by hand. According to Mr Pearce, the handling improves the flavour of the bread. Prove for 15 mins. and put into the moulding machine to shape and remove some of the air. Place into tins and prove for 30-40 mins.

Bake for 1 hour at 460-480 F, placing tins towards the top of the oven to give a dark black crusty top.

SAFFRON BUNS

From Mr Doug Lewis at the Hot Bloomers Bakery, Callington

Ingredients for ferment
1¹/₂ (840 ml) pints warm water
1 lb (450 g) strong white flour
1 oz (25 g) sugar
3 oz (75 g) whey powder
2 tsp liquid saffron
¹/₂ pint (250 ml) eggs
8 oz (225 g) yeast
Dry Ingredients
3¹/₂ lb (1.575 kg) flour
7 oz (200 g) sugar
1 oz (25 g) salt
10 oz (300 g) white fat
1 lb (450 g) margarine
Fruit
2 lb 4 oz (1 kg) currants
1 lb 4 oz (560 g) sultanas
8 oz (225 g) mixed peel
The above quantities make a 5 lb (2.250kg) lump of dough, which can be used for buns or saffron loaves.
Method Place water in bucket and add saffron; whisk together before adding the rest of the ingredients, eggs last. Whisk again and ferment for ¹/₂ hour. Place the dry ingredients in mixing bowl and add the ferment. Mix in mixer, slow speed with a hook for 15 mins, then add fruit. Scale and mould into 36 small buns, which are then rounded and moulded into 18 larger buns. Or the mixture can be used to make 1 lb or 2 lb loaves.
Bake at 350 F for 12 mins. for buns or 30 mins. for cakes.

RUSTIC LOAF

from Mr Brian O'Donnell at The Cottage Bakery, Gunnislake

The loaf is dark in colour, round and flat. The combination of seeds and cashew nuts gives a satisfying taste; one slice is almost a meal in itself.

Ingredients

2 lb (900 g) untreated white flour
2 lb (900 g) rye meal
3 lb (1.350 kg) Harvest flour (a granary type of flour)
2 oz (50 g) salt
2 oz (50 g) improver (E300) or Vit C.
2 oz (50 g) poppy seeds
2 oz (50 g) sesame seeds
2 oz (50 g) sunflower seeds
4 oz (110 g) cashew nuts
8 oz (225 g) yeast
Approx. $3^{1}/_{4}$ pints (1.8 litres) of water

Method Mix all ingredients together, mould and shape by hand and allow to prove for $^{3}/_{4}$ hour.

Bake for 30 mins at 250 F.

LISKEARD

THREE bakeries serve the town of Liskeard and although the names of the loaves are rather dull, certain regional characteristics can be discerned.

It seems that customers in Liskeard dislike change and prefer to use the terms that they know. Brown loaves are still called wheatmeal here, despite Government categories to the contrary, and a batch can mean almost anything, either a round cob or a bloomer shape. A tray batch is unique to the area, a small bloomer shaped loaf with soft sides, and the flat batch baked by one bakery is round like a cob but lower and flatter. Tin loaves are called uprights and sandwich loaves can be long or short undertins.

Here you can buy crusty rolls known as hard bakes, yeast buns are white or yellow dough buns, and there are two kinds of splits. One is sold for everyday use and a richer version called a Cornish split has more fat and sugar. At one time, strips of saffron bun were sold by weight in the Liskeard area and called pounders, a distinctive variation on feast buns and tea treats.

A wide and interesting selection of bread is on sale at Blakes the Master Bakers, Dean Street, Liskeard. The bread is displayed in old fashioned baskets, and the bakery which dates back 100 years, is at the rear of the shop. As well as the tray batch, rye bread is baked with Bavarian rye and proved in baskets, showing the attractive markings on the finished loaf. The mixed grain loaf looks like a small Hovis, but is made with sunflower and sesame seeds, and the caraway wholemeal loaf is made from a wholemeal dough with caraway seeds added. The appearance and shape of this loaf could be said to be medieval: round and flat with a grill of crosses indented on top.

CARAWAY WHOLEMEAL LOAF

From Mr J.E. Blake at Blake's the Master Bakers, Liskeard

This is a basic wholemeal dough.

Ingredients
70 lbs (31.75 kg) stoneground wholemeal flour
1$^1/_2$ lbs (680 g) salt
12 oz (350 g) vegetable fat
2 lb (900 g) yeast
40 lbs (18 kgs) water
1 oz (25 g) caraway seeds for every 6 loaves.

Method Add water to dry ingredients and mix on 2nd speed in spiral mixer for 10 mins. (6 mins. fast and 4 slow). Allow to prove for 20 mins. Divide the dough by hand, adding the caraway seeds at this stage. Rest for 10-12 mins, then mould again by hand, making the distinctive cross marking on top of the loaf. Allow to prove for a further 30-40 mins.

Bake at 440 F for 40-45 mins.

LOOE TO POLRUAN

THE batch in Looe would be called a bloomer in many other bakeries in the county and as in Liskeard, a brown loaf is still called a wheatmeal. A speckled loaf, with sunflower seeds, is made at Looe Bakery and here too they bake a sandwich loaf in brown flour as well as white.

Nearby, Palfrey's Bakery has a good display of bread, with some old-fashioned lines; many of their cakes are made with Hovis flour, for example, and these are popular with older customers. The family have been baking in the town for many years and the deep, gas-fired ovens have been in use for at least twenty-five years. Mr R.T. Palfrey gives his recipe for the attractive *milk plait* sold at Palfrey's Bakery.

Both Polperro and Polruan are fortunate in having their own bakeries. Travelling to Polruan is like travelling to the end of the world, a long way from anywhere. When one does arrive, however, the reward is to find a real village bakery in one of the steeply sided streets, a stone's throw away from the Harbour. Run by a young, enthusiastic couple, Mr and Mrs Tony Minall, from Banbury, the shop offers speciality and novelty breads to customer orders — pigs, frogs, horses and hedgehogs, for example. Unusually, *French sticks* are made with *flèche d'or* French flour and the milk bread is baked with a touch of malt. Here, the bloomer is sold in the long traditional shape and is not called a batch, as in Looe. A popular recipe is given for *soft grain bread*, baked with cracked wheat and vinegar.

Polperro attracts the tourists and the bakery run by Mr Alan Butters is part of the local scene. A large, prominent sign advertising Cornish pasties baked in coal-fired ovens, tempts the tourists to venture into the shop, which is a listed building and cannot be altered or expanded and has been a bakery for about 150 years. No doubt the restricted selling area and low doorway are an added attraction, however.

103

Many people claim that the coal-fired ovens give the bread a distinct flavour and until last year Mr Butters used the ovens to roast customers' turkeys at Christmas.

Names in Polperro are fairly standard, perhaps to keep in step with the tourists who flock into the village during the summer months. A batch is a bloomer shape and occasionally Mr Butters bakes a muesli loaf, known as a warrior loaf, from a basic white dough with a mixture of seeds and grains to give a speckled appearance.

MILK PLAIT

From Mr R. T. Palfrey, Palfrey's Bakery, East Looe

The loaf can be round or plaited and seeded with poppy seeds or left plain.

Ingredients

2½ lb (1.125 kg) white bread flour
¾ oz (20 g) salt
½ oz (15 g) sugar
¾ oz (20 g) fat
1 oz (25 g) milk powder
1½ oz (40 g) yeast
Approx. 1¼ pint (650 ml) water

Method Sieve flour, salt, sugar and milk powder together. Rub in fat and make a bay. Add the yeast to the water, whisk and add to flour. Knead and allow to stand for 1 hour with a dough temp. of 78 F. Knock back and stand for a further 30 mins. Scale and mould into plaits or whatever other shapes are required. Prove in the steam prover for 20 mins.

Bake at 375 F for 20 mins, on trays at the bottom of the oven.

SOFT GRAIN BREAD

Two recipes from Mr Tony Minall at Polruan Bakery

A soft loaf with cracked wheat, increasingly popular with customers. Vinegar is an unusual ingredient.

Ingredients

2 lb (900 g) white bread flour
4 oz (110 g) cracked wheat
1 pint (560 ml) water
2 oz (50 g) yeast
2 oz (50 g) vegetable fat
1 oz (25 g) vinegar
$^1/_2$ oz (15 g) salt

Method Sieve dry ingredients together and, using small mixer, mix in yeast and water. Leave to ferment for 1 hour. Scale off into 2 lb (900 g) and 1 lb (450 g) weights. Prove in the tin for 40 mins. Bake at 450 F for 25-30 mins.

FRENCH STICK

French flèche d'or flour is used for this recipe, giving an authentic flavour.

Ingredients

$4^1/_2$ lb (2.025 kg) white flèche d'or flour
$1^1/_2$ oz (40 g) salt
2 oz (50 g) yeast
$2^1/_2$ lb (1.125 kg) water
$1^1/_2$ oz (40 g) bread improver

Method Dough temp. 80 F. Add water and yeast to dry ingredients and mix for 10-15 mins. Ferment for just 10 mins. Scale off into 1 lb (450 g) weights, rest for 10-15 mins and then mould into long French sticks. Prove slowly for 60-80 mins, then make cuts across the dough before baking at 430 F for 20-25 mins.

SALTASH AND CAWSAND

BAKERIES appear in the most unlikely places and none more so than in the narrow, stone streets of Cawsand, thronged with tourists in the summer and deserted in winter. An example of a real Cornish fishing village, Cawsand is steeped in history, at a stand-still with time. The bakery here is run by a young dedicated couple, Mr and Mrs David and Cathy Mayhew, who have been baking in Cawsand since 1988.

The names of the loaves seem unaffected by the proximity of Plymouth and are quite individual. A Danish, for example, is like a large bloomer but covered with cracked wheat and poppy seeds. For this, weekend visitors seem to like a dark, well-cooked loaf, whereas mid-week customers prefer a lighter bake. At weekends, the bakery produce a Turkestan loaf, made with soft grains, sesame seeds and honey. As well as being a healthy loaf, it is also recommended by dentists, as the soft grains do not damage the teeth.

Mr R. Black runs the nearby Saltash Bakery and he has been in the trade for the past 35 years. Although the range of bread baked is extensive, the names are straightforward. A tin loaf, however, comes in three varieties: a long split tin, an upright split tin or even a square split tin. Sandwich loaves can be square or long. Cobs and batches in Saltash are similar in shape and size, but a cob is a round white loaf whereas a batch is brown and seeded. Attractive, circular bread rings are also baked. Rolls come in a variety of sizes, small, large or jumbo, and when elongated they are known as points.

TURKESTAN LOAF

*Information supplied by Spillers Premier Products, Cambridge
and recipe baked at the Cawsand bakery*

The loaf has been sold in the Plymouth area since the late
1970s and is now mainly baked by the larger supermarkets
with in-store bakery facilities.

'Turkestan is a remote region of Asiatic Russia, and has
been the home of the Turkomana tribes since Biblical times.
The nomadic Turkoman, as shown in the Turkestan symbol,
were and indeed still are, shepherds, horse breeders and wool
merchants.

'The Turkoman staple diet consists of unleavened Turkestan
bread and green tea, and is thought to contribute to their
long life expectancy — some Turkomans are known to live
for over 100 years.

'Turkestan bread is based on the traditional recipes of
Turkestan.'

Ingredients, which include the special Turkestan mixes:
Water, wholemeal flour, flour, kibbled wheat, wheat flakes,
wheat protein, kibbled malted wheat, cracked rye, salt, honey,
soya flour, yeast, barley flakes, sesame seeds, soya bran, dried
glucose syrup, emulsifier (E472e), flour improver, ascorbic
Acid (Vit.C)

Recommended Bakery Recipe for 1 lb (400g) Tin Bread
68 lbs (32 kg) Wholemeal bread flour
34 lbs (16 kg) Turkestan no soak grain mix
34 lbs (16 kg) Turkestan bread and roll concentrate
2 lbs 4 oz (1.2 kg) yeast
75 lbs (35.2 kg) water
Dough temp. 28-29 C
Ingredients for 207 loaves

Method High speed for 3 mins. or spiral for 2 mins. on slow
and 6-8 mins. on fast. Conventional mixers 20-25 mins.
Before baking, roll dough in Turkestan no-soak grain mix.

THE HISTORY OF BREAD

THE Egyptians discovered sour-dough leavening (dough left until it has soured) and invented the bee-hive oven. Setting a precedent, they gave brown bread to the peasants, keeping the white bread for the aristocrats.

The Greeks perfected the art of bread-making, adding all manner of ingredients, while the Romans introduced commercial baking.

The preference for white bread continued into medieval times, with the lords and ladies eating the white bread themselves, but then distributing the trenchers or plates, made of brown bread, to the poor. Later, in the eighteenth century, additives were mixed with the flour to improve the whiteness. Some of these were poisonous; white lead and alum, for example, continued to be used until they were banned by law, towards the end of the nineteenth century.

Today we still eat more white bread than brown, but wholemeal bread is gaining in popularity. Soft grain bread, a form of white bread with added wheat grains and flakes, is also taking an increasing share of the market. It is thought to offer a good compromise between white and brown bread and is especially favoured by children. Wholewheat flour is generally thought to be more nutritious, with more fibre and vitamins, although white flour contains 75% of the wheat grain and is a useful source of calcium. Present-day legislation allows certain chemicals and other additives to be used with bread flour (apart from wholemeal), to ensure an adequate supply of vitamins and minerals, making bread a healthy and wholesome diet.

THE BASICS OF BREAD MAKING

BREAD consists of flour, yeast, salt and water. To these basic ingredients a host of optional extras can be added: nuts, seeds or fruit, as well as milk powder, sugar, eggs or fat. The water is added to moisten the flour and the resulting dough is then kneaded, allowed to prove or rise and finally baked in the oven.

Bread making is above all fun and the baker enjoys using his discretion in baking bread to suit both his own and his customers' tastes. Each loaf is a work of art created by the cook and is an example of his or her particular culinary skill.

INGREDIENTS

Flour

This can be white, wholemeal, brown or granary. **Strong white flour** must be used, owing to the high gluten content. The best and strongest flour comes from Canada, where the warmer and longer days produce a high gluten yield. The Spring wheat grown in this country gives us suitably strong flour, but with less gluten. Strong white flour contains 72%-74% of the whole grain; it can be bleached but more and more bakers are choosing unbleached flours for their bread. Potassium bromate has recently been prohibited as a flour improver, but other permitted additives under Government regulations help to ensure that white flour provides us with an adequate intake of minerals and vitamins.

At the other end of the spectrum, **wholemeal flour**, as the name suggests, is flour with the whole of the wheat included (bran, endosperm, wheat germ) with no additives or subtractions. Used on its own for bread making, it produces rather a heavy, close textured loaf, which some people prefer. The addition of other forms of flour tends to lighten the loaf in colour and weight. The oil from the wheat germ is incorporated into the flour and consequently it does not keep well and customers are advised to buy small quantities and not to keep the flour for too long in the store cupboard.

Brown flour is the modern name for wheatmeal flour, which is wholemeal flour with the bran extracted, usually containing 85-90% of the wholegrain. Many people consider this to be the ideal brown bread, giving colour and lightness. **Farmhouse flour** contains about 80% of the whole wheat.

Granary flour is now the proprietary name (Rank-Hovis) for brown flour with added malted wheat flakes. Other companies use different names for similar flours, Harvester or Cobber flour for example. Legally, the bread should be called by the name of the flour, but in practice customers invariably ask for a granary loaf.

Stoneground flour has been milled in the old-fashioned way, between two stones, usually granite, rather than by the modern steel sheet-rollers. A few really traditional wind or water millers still exist and their names can be obtained from 'The Traditional Cornmillers Guild', Maud Foster Mill, Boston, Lincs. There are no such mills in Cornwall, the nearest is in Harbertonford, near Totnes in Devon. Bakers' flour is generally bought in bulk from the larger flour manufacturers who use roller milling, although it is interesting to note that many of the smaller bakeries are turning to stoneground flour. There is a distinct difference in flavour, but the choice is a matter of individual taste.

A wide variety of other flours can be used in bread making, either alone or mixed with white, brown or wholemeal flour. Perhaps **rye flour** is the best known, used widely on the Continent, particularly in Germany, and becoming increasingly popular here. On its own, rye flour produces a heavy, flat, dense loaf which does not keep well so that it is best to incorporate rye with other flours. Similarly **barley flour** and **oatmeal** need to be used in conjunction with other flours, and baking powder or bicarbonate of soda are usually used for rising, rather than yeast. In the past both flours were used quite extensively, particularly in Scotland.

Cornmeal is ground from maize, the yellow corn on the cob; and cornflour is finely-ground cornmeal. Both are popular in the United States and Latin America. The flour contains a high proportion of starch, as does **rice flour**. They are useful for dusting loaves before baking and when a sticky, fatty dough is being handled. Many other flours can be utilized successfully, such as **potato flour**, **chickpea flour**, **soya flour** which is especially low in starch and rich in protein, **buckwheat flour** and **semolina meal**.

Writing in 1857, Eliza Acton in her masterpiece *The English Bread Book*, lists a variety of other ingredients: parsnips, beetroot, French beans, millet and sago. Other additions such as sunflower or pumpkin seeds, poppy seeds, all the spices and many kinds of fruit are acceptable.

Yeast

Everyone has their own predilection as far as yeast is concerned. Bakers generally use fresh yeast, bought in bulk from one of the manufacturers specializing in the product. Housewives seem to prefer the convenience of dried yeast, which is easily stored and readily available. It must be remembered too that dried yeast is twice as strong as fresh yeast and half the quantity should be used. Gaining in popularity is the relative newcomer, easy-blend dried yeast. Here, the yeast can be added directly to the flour, without being reconstituted in liquid first. Not only does this save time, but the results are just as good as with fresh or dried yeast. Extreme temperatures kill yeast and so tepid or hand hot liquid must be used when mixing the dough. Equally, the proving temperature should be warm rather than too hot or cold.

Salt

A casual sprinkling of salt into the dry ingredients does not always produce the desired results. Contrary to popular belief, the quantity of salt does affect the final product. Salt is not only responsible for the taste of the bread but it also helps to retain the moisture in the loaf, while too much salt produces a hard outer crust and can kill the yeast. Generally, the shorter the rising time for the bread, the more yeast and less salt is needed. Care should be taken in weighing out the correct quantities of salt: just less than $^1/_2$ oz for every 1 lb of flour.

Sugar

Although sugar is generally regarded as food for the yeast and essential to bread making, it is only really necessary when reconstituting dried yeast in liquid. Too much sugar can kill the yeast and produces an unpleasant taste. Brown sugar is often recommended for wholemeal bread, to give extra flavour, although other sweeteners such as honey, treacle or syrup can also be used.

Fat

Bread can be made quite successfully without fat, although when added it helps to enrich the dough and the colour and volume of the loaf are improved. Fat enriched loaves are generally softer and keep longer. Butter may seem extravagant, but is regarded as the best fat to use for rich doughs, some bakers make a habit of indulging their customers with butter instead of margarine for Christmas or Easter baking. Lard is added more frequently to plainer breads although oil works equally well. Sometimes the fat has to be melted, in which case it should be cooled before being added to the dough.

Liquid

Water is generally used in bread making. Soft water is said to be preferable to hard and as the taste of water varies from place to place, regional flavours are obtained.

Milk is equally successful, although it is best combined with water in the proportions of one part milk to two parts of water. Milk is said to prolong the life of the loaf, owing to the fat content, and generally helps to improve the crumb. Bread can only be termed 'milk bread' when full cream milk is used. Other milk-related products can be added to the dry ingredients just as successfully: yogurt, buttermilk, sour cream and even clotted cream. Some West Country recipes specify clotted cream; for example, with Sally Lunns made from a light, sweet bread, shining and golden on top and pale underneath. The name is a corruption of '*sol' et lune*'. Beer, malt and fruit juices can also be used to help moisten and flavour the dough.

Miscellaneous additions
Dried fruit is called for in many recipes, although small quantities of fresh fruit can also be added for variety. Eggs enrich the dough and syrup, treacle and honey add sweetness. An infinite variety of spices, flavourings and essences can be incorporated, according to taste. Lemons are particularly refreshing and Eliza Acton recommends ginger. Her recipe for Ginger Loaf appears in *The English Bread Book*, although she cautions that over indulgence causes constipation!

Saffron
Saffron is widely used by bakers in Cornwall and the bright yellow loaves and buns create colour and interest in a shop window. According to legend, saffron was introduced into Cornwall by the Phoenecians who landed on the Cornish coast in search of tin. Although there is little or no historical evidence to support this theory, culinary history is enhanced and enlivened by such myths and it would be a shame to dismiss the tale altogether.

Saffron is harvested from the stigmas of the purple crocus, *Crocus sativus* and the stigmas are then spread out on trays and dried over charcoal fires. The deep red threads make a yellow dye when steeped in liquid. For baking, the strands of saffron are soaked overnight in warm milk or water and the liquid, with or without the strands, is then incorporated into the dough. If the strands are mixed in, the baker can then prove that he has used real saffron and not an inferior yellow dye.

The word saffron comes from the Arabic, *zafaran*, meaning yellow, and is now only grown commercially in Kashmir and Spain. At one time, it was grown in this country, hence the name Saffron Walden in Essex. A pilgrim returning from the Crusades in the fourteenth century is said to have introduced saffron to the area by hiding a crocus bulb in the head of his staff. Cultivation in Saffron Walden was at the height of popularity during the sixteenth century and then gradually declined. Now the only autumn crocuses to be seen in the area are in the Saffron Walden Museum.

Saffron has had a wide variety of culinary uses over the centuries. As well as a seasoning and spice, followers of Buddha dyed their robes with saffron and the Greeks and Romans used it to perfume rooms. Herbalists recommend saffron as a cure for all manner of ailments, although they warn that an overdose could cause death by laughter! Saffron has a mention in the *Book of Solomon*, chap. 4, verse 14: 'Your two cheeks are an orchard of pomegranates . . . spikenard and saffron' (spikenard is a fragrant oil or ointment), and the clown in Shakespeare's *Winter's Tale* act 4, sc.11, says 'I must have saffron to colour the warden pies'. (Pies made with pears and flavoured with saffron).

Cornwall and the West Country, Northumberland and Ireland still bake with saffron. Why saffron has been retained in these areas is difficult to surmise. There is evidence that the Romans were in Cornwall and it could be their legacy. Various wills and documents refer to 'saffron meadows', as at Fowey in the seventeenth century. In 1871 there is a reference to saffron growing in Launcells, near Bude.

Saffron is the most expensive spice in the world. 150,000 flowers are needed to produce one kilo of dried saffron.

THE METHODS OF BREAD MAKING

Mixing, kneading and proving

FIRST of all, successful bread requires a warm temperature for the room, the utensils and all the ingredients. The liquid and yeast are added to the dry ingredients and after mixing, the dough is kneaded until smooth and elastic. Most experts agree that this stage is essential: kneading adds air to the bread and ensures that all the ingredients are thoroughly blended. The dough is then covered with oiled cling-film or a tea-towel and left to rise or prove until well risen or doubled in size. Rising time depends on the room temperature and the richness of the dough. A warm place enables the dough to rise quickly, whereas a cooler room delays and controls the growth of the yeast. Richer doughs take longer to prove and usually benefit from a cooler temperature. Some recipes specify a second kneading or 'knocking back' to re-invigorate the yeast, before the final rising and baking.

Glazing and finishing

The final dough can be brushed with milk to give a golden crust, water to make the crust crispy or egg to make it shine. Seeds, nuts or grains scattered over the loaf prior before baking also give an attractive and unusual finish.

Cuts on the crust

Slashes and cuts on the dough give the loaves identity. Tin loaves are cut during the rising, giving time for the cuts to expand as the dough rises, whereas oven-bottom baked breads are slashed just before baking.

Baking

Bread is either baked in a tin, or shaped and moulded and then baked on the sole of the oven or on a heavy baking sheet. The temperature must be high, to kill the yeast and prevent the bread from rising further. Longer baking gives the loaf a darker appearance. The loaf is done when it is well risen, golden brown and sounds hollow when tapped on the base. Modern bakery ovens are usually electric, whereas in the past coke or oil fired ovens were used. A steamy oven produces bread with a good crust and many professional bakers inject a burst of steam into the ovens at the start of baking time to improve the crust.

IN CONCLUSION

THE shape and style of a loaf is said to reflect the society that bakes and then consumes it. Long French sticks are designed for the table, easily sliced or broken by hand, with cross cuts that give a crisp outer crust. Soft Vienna bread is eaten in Austria's musical city, sophisticated and light, while in contrast, dark rye bread has grown up as part of the peasant diet in rural Russia and many other European countries.

In the British Isles, Ireland is well known for potato bread and soda bread, Scotland for oat cakes and Wales for bara brith. Cornwall has heavy cake, pasties and saffron bread, the latter of interest to tourists who are curious about the history and content of these bright yellow loaves. The county has lost so many traditional industries and customs but still our pasties and saffron buns remain, to remind us of our past, of the pilchards and the tin mines, and to sustain our newest industry, tourism.

BIBLIOGRAPHY

Acton, Eliza: *The English Bread Book*, London, Longmans Green, 1857

Bailey, Adrian: *The Blessings of Bread*, Paddington Press, 1975

Beeton, Isabella: *Mrs Beeton's Book of Household Management*, London, 1861

Christian Glynn: *Bread and Yeast Cookery*, Macdonald Educational Ltd, 1978

David, Elizabeth: *English Bread and Yeast Cookery*, Allen Lane, 1977

Fitzgibbon, Theodora: *A Taste of England*, Pan Books, 1986

Hartley, Dorothy: *Food in England*, London, Macdonald, 1954

Norwak, Mary: *The W.I. Book of Bread and Buns*, W.I. Books, 1984

Pellowe, Susan: *Saffron and Currants*, Renard Productions, 1989

Saffron Walden Museum: *The Saffron Crocus*

The W.I. and Michael Smith: *A Cook's Tour of Britain*, W.I. Books, 1984

Although it has not been possible to contact Adrain Bailey, grateful acknowledgment is made for the quotation from *The Blessings of Bread*, Paddington Press, 1975. Also, I would like to acknowledge the helpful information received from the Flour Advisory Bureau, London

INDEX